NEALE DONALD WALSCH

WHEN EVERYTHING CHANGES

CHANGE EVERYTHING

IN A TIME
OF TURMOIL,
A PATHWAY
TO PEACE

an *EmNin* book

When Everything Changes, Change Everything
In a Time of Turmoil, a Pathway to Peace

Neale Donald Walsch

Cover design by Frame25 Productions
Cover art by Palto c/o Shutterstock.com and
Andresr c/o Shutterstock.com

EmNin Books
PMB 1144
1257 Siskiyou Blvd.
Ashland, OR 97520
e-mail: emninbooks@aol.com

ISBN 978-1-57174-606-1

Distributed by:
Hampton Roads Publishing Company, Inc.
1125 Stoney Ridge Road
Charlottesville, VA 22902

434-296-2772
fax: 434-296-5096
e-mail: hrpc@hrpub.com
www.hrpub.com

10 9 8 7 6 5 4 3 2 1
Printed on acid-free paper in Canada

Please sit down.

No, really.

Please.

Sit down.

There's a better than even chance you're reading these first few words standing up (in a bookstore someplace, or maybe in someone's home), scanning these lines to see if you want to read any further.

If you are, please sit down. You're not going to want to read the first few paragraphs and then just walk away. You're going to want more time with what's written here. So "steal" as many moments as you can with this book before deciding whether to buy it—because I want you to know what you're getting yourself into.

This book is not just a book. It is meant to be a conversation during which we will conduct an extraordinary investigation into how life works at the mental and spiritual level, out of which will emerge a surprising revelation about ways in which we can change our experience of change itself—which means, of course, our experience of *life*.

The conversation we are about to have will thus offer you a pathway to get help and to find peace if you are struggling right now with *changes* in your life. Why I wanted you to sit down is that I wanted you to be in a better position to hear all of this, to really take it in. What I'm going to share with you here is not something that you can just pick up "on the run," as it were, in little snippets and snatches and bits of reading grabbed here and there. This is a book you're going to want to sit down with.

I also wanted you to be seated when you hear the news. So here it is. Sitting or standing, ready or not, here it is:

The changes in your life are not going to stop.

If you're thinking about riding things out for a while, waiting for things to settle down a bit, you may be in for a surprise. There's going to be no "settling down." Things are going to be in a constant state of upheaval on this planet and in your own life for a good while now. Actually . . . yes, well, I might as well tell you. . . . actually, *forever*.

Change is *what is*—and there is no way to change that. . . .

What can be changed is the way you deal with change,
and the way you're changed by change.

That's what this book is about.

We are going to be talking here about how to deal with major change, not just minor change. I mean change that emerges from collapse, calamity, and catastrophe—or at least what we label as these. So if your life is collapsing right now, if you're in the midst of a calamity, if a catastrophe has occurred, what you're going to find here could save your life. I mean, emotionally. But heck, you know what? Maybe even physically.

Here you will be given Nine Changes That Can Change Everything. This little list will alter all that appears in your reality. Unless it does not. The choice will be yours. But it is a list that you may at least want to read. You may at least want to find out what it's all about.

I hope that you will make these Nine Changes as quickly as possible. Not just because the changes in life that you are experiencing (that we *all* are experiencing) are not going to stop, but also because the *pace* of change is only going to *increase*.

Someone noted a few years ago that it was possible for my great-grandfather to live an entire lifetime without having anything come along that seriously challenged his worldview, because very little happened that he heard about that altered his understanding of how things were.

My grandfather had a different experience. He was able to live thirty or forty years, but not much longer, before some new piece of information was unveiled that seriously confronted his notion of the world. Perhaps half a dozen times during his life such a major event or development occurred that he heard about.

In my father's day that window of change dropped to only fifteen or twenty years. That's about as long as my dad could hold on to his ideas about life and how it works and what is true about everything. Sooner or later something would happen to disrupt his whole mental construction and require him to alter his thoughts and concepts.

In my own life span that time has been reduced to just five to eight years.

In the lifetime of my children it will be reduced to something like two years—and possibly less. And in the lifetime of *their* children it could be reduced to thirty or forty *weeks*.

This is no exaggeration. You can see the trend. Social scientists say that the rate of change is increasing exponentially. In the time of my great-grandchildren the period of time between changes will be reduced to days. And then, perhaps even hours.

In truth, we are already there—and have *always* been there. For in actuality, nothing has ever remained the same for even a moment. Everything is in motion, and if we define change as the altering of configurations, we see that change is the natural order of things. So we've been living in a constant swirl of change from the beginning.

What is different now is the amount of *time* that it takes for us to notice the changes that are always occurring. Our ability to communicate globally about everything within seconds is what has changed the way we experience change. The speed of our communications is catching up with the speed of our alterations. This condition in itself sponsors an increase in the rate of change.

Today our languages and expressions change overnight, our customs and styles change by the season, our beliefs and understandings and even some of our most deeply held convictions change not with, but *within*, each generation.

Because change is happening all around us and within us so rapidly, what is needed now is a guidebook, an "operator's manual" for human beings facing dramatically shifting life realities. This book is, therefore, more than a collection of anecdotes or "real life stories" about people who have gone through changes in their life, or a once-over-lightly treatment of something that deserves deeper exploration. The text that follows offers some peeks at the experience of others (including my own), because there can be value in that, but it also provides a much-needed explanation of the mental and spiritual *basis* of change—and specific instructions on how to use mental and spiritual tools to *change the way change changes you.*

What the Nine Changes empower us to do is not stop change (I hope I've already made the point that this is impossible) or even slow the rate of change, but rather, make a quantum leap in our *approach* to change, in our ways of *dealing* with it—and in our ways of *creating* it.

One final word. The ideas here are based in ancient wisdom, modern science, everyday psychology, practical metaphysics, and contemporary spirituality. The invitation here presumes that Divinity exists, that life has a purpose, that human beings have a soul, that our body is something we have and not something we are, and that the mind is under our control at all times.

A rejection of any one of these notions removes the underpinning from much of what is shared here. On the other hand, if these concepts feel valid to you, you could be holding in your hand the most useful, the most helpful, the most powerful book you have read in a very long time.

NINE CHANGES THAT CAN CHANGE EVERYTHING

1. Change your decision to "go it alone"

2. Change your choice of emotions

3. Change your choice of thoughts

4. Change your choice of truths

5. Change your idea about Change Itself

6. Change your idea about why Change occurs

7. Change your idea about future Change

8. Change your idea about life

9. Change your identity

AUTHOR'S NOTE

THE EXPLORATION THAT FOLLOWS is divided into two parts. The first deals with the physical aspects of how we experience change, while the second deals with the metaphysical aspects. In other words, we'll look first at how the mind works, then at how the soul works.

By mastering both aspects of our being we remember not only how to think, but *what* to think. What I'm clear about now is that the mind is a tool, a mechanism, and the soul provides the fuel for that machine. The less fuel you use, the more inefficiently the engine will operate. On the other hand, if your soul *fills* your mind with spiritual energy, you will be Mind-Full—and the workings of this engine can produce miracles.

PART ONE
The Mechanics of the Mind

*And how knowing about that can help you change
your experience of the change you're experiencing*

1.

THE JUST-IN-TIME BOOK

IF SOMETHING IMPORTANT around you is changing right now, I'm sorry.

I know how comforting it can be to finally get some things into place. I also know how it feels to yearn to have those things *stay* in place. And I know how upsetting it can be when they don't, when they won't, when they just *can't*.

It is obviously more than "upsetting" if what has changed are situations and conditions affecting your SAFETY.

If you suddenly find yourself without a livelihood, unable to find work, desperately behind in your bills, maybe even losing your home, you are dealing with more than just the feeling that "things have changed." You're dealing with feeling that "everything is lost." This is not simply a feeling of being disrupted or discombobulated, this is a feeling of being *threatened*.

Even if you're not facing change on that order of calamity, but a significant change in your life nonetheless, *threat* could be very much a part of your experience. Most of us feel that our very way of life is threatened when we face any kind of major change, especially if it is around the Big Three:

RELATIONSHIP
MONEY
HEALTH

If one of these things is changing, it can be very challenging. It *two* of these three are changing, it can be incredibly difficult. If *all three* are changing at the same time, it can be utterly devastating.

I know this.

I've lived it.

All three. I've lived through all three. At once.

Talk about feeling *threatened* . . .

. . . I broke my neck in a car accident (Health), had to stop working through months of rehabilitation while an insurance company tried to figure out every way possible to reduce or eliminate compensation (Money), all the while I was working through the pain of separation from my life partner and our children as our lives dramatically changed course (Relationship).

Talk about feeling *threatened* . . .

I wound up homeless for a year, living in the weather, walking the streets panhandling for pocket change and collecting soda cans and beer bottles to scrape together enough money to eat (some days it didn't go so well), with a sleeping bag and a tent, two pair of jeans, three shirts, and a few odds and ends as my only possessions.

I know about losing one's sense of safety. I know about standing by helplessly and watching life fall apart, changing utterly and completely in two weeks' time.

Yeah, I know about that. Trust me.

And I know a little something about how to deal with it, too. Not that I did such a good job at the time, mind you, but then again, this book is about what I've learned since.

We're going to talk here about what I've picked up from some very authoritative sources on how to deal with *change*. Because that's what this is all about, at the bottom line. It feels like we're dealing with collapse, calamity, catastrophe . . . but those are all outward effects created by a single cause: Change. Something is not the way it was before. Something has been altered. Irrevocably, immeasurably, fundamentally, and absolutely.

A lady who is going through huge turmoil in her life sent me an e-mail today. She is aware that I'm writing this book and she said, "I don't know that I would even have identified what is happening to me as 'change.' When you are in the middle of it, when everything is falling apart around you, you can't identify it or name it as 'change.' It feels more like THE END . . . everything you know is coming to an end and there is *nothing after*. If you'd asked me before I heard about your book if I was experiencing change, I would not have defined it that way. I don't know what I would have called it, other than to say that life was ruined, finished."

This lady, whose name is Leah and who gave me permission to quote her in this book, added something very insightful.

"Change is scary," she said, "but that's different from feeling like it's 'Game Over.' I looked up 'change' in the dictionary.

Change indicates that something new is coming. This is a very different perspective from what some people (who are facing calamity in their lives) might have, and it might be helpful to first assist them to even identify with the fact that what is happening is CHANGE; to understand the very definition of change."

That's good, Leah. That's good stuff right there. So I tore apart the first chapter that I had written and came back with this one. I realized Leah was right. So I'm going to define CHANGE as I am using the word:

> Change is the shifting of any circumstance, situation, or condition, physical or nonphysical, in such a way that the original is rendered not merely different from what it was, but altered so radically as to make it utterly unrecognizable and impossible to return to anything resembling its former state.

In other words, we are talking about a major shift here; we are not talking about changing one's clothing or the menu for lunch or the evening's TV agenda. We are talking about life-changing events—the kind that hurt, the kind that do damage, the kind that kill dreams and ruin plans and disrupt futures—and we are talking about *healing* them with equally life-changing events. We are saying that when everything changes, sometimes the best thing to do is to change everything. Not only everything in the physical, but everything in the *non-physical.* This would include your emotions, your thoughts, even your truths.

We're talking about a complete overhaul here, from top to bottom, inside and out. After all, your life has been turned darned near inside out anyway, so why not finish the job? Only now, in the way that *you* want it to feel, rather than in the way that it feels you are being forced to accept. . . .

As we embark on this exploration I hope you can feel that I understand at least a little of what's going on with you, so that you know that you're not hearing about all this from somebody who has no idea what you're going through—some "fix-it guru" sermonizing at you from the mountaintop who has never been anywhere near where you are right now. I hope you can feel that even if nothing else is going right in your life, your having picked up this book is at least one good thing. *One good thing has happened today.*

We can start with that. We can begin from there. We're going to stand side by side, you and I, and put your whole life back together again—in a new way, in an even better way.

Dare I promise that? Well, I'm saying, "Let's try." Let's see what we can do. You've got nothing to lose, right? So let's try. Let's make your having picked up this book be not only one good thing that happened *today*, but one of the best things that's happened *in your life!*

What do you say? Want to do it? Want to try?

If you're too tired, too beaten down, too exhausted from the battle of life to even try, would you just do *this* . . . ? Would you just *try* to try?

If you'll try to try, I think we can make it. And I'll promise you this. You don't have to go any faster than you want, any faster than you feel comfortable with.

I'm going to give you lots of stopping points, lots of breathing spaces, so that you can "take a break" whenever you'd like. There's nothing worse than a Feeling-Good-Is-As-Easy-As-Pie book when you're experiencing just the opposite. I hate those. I hate those

Rah!

Rah!

Ciss-boom-bah!

books. *Yeah, right, just throw up a cheer and everything will be better*, I say to myself. *Sure.* Then I start feeling even worse, because I can't seem to get it right—even though the person writing the book says it's so easy. . . .

So let's see if we agree on something here. *It's not easy.* Not without the tools. And who has the tools? What school taught Calamity 101? Where was the class in Elements of Change in Modern Day Life? So dealing with major change, monumental change, has not been easy for most of us.

Yet it can be. You can undergo change, stand in the middle of catastrophe, and be okay. You can be *very* okay. I know that feels counterintuitive, but it happens to be true.

That's all I wanted to tell you in these first few moments we're together. I just wanted to give you a reason for going on. And I don't mean just with this book. You know what I mean.

Okay. That may be enough to think about for now. You can go on with your reading if you want, but you don't have to. I mean, this is a perfect place to stop, to put the book down now and take a break.

Like I said, I've designed the book with lots of stopping points. Lots of places to just "take a breath" and be with your-self and the ideas we're looking at. You'll find these breathing spaces not just at the end of chapters, but right in the middle of them. (I hate that feeling that you just want to at least make it to the end of the chapter or you feel like some kind of dropout, some kind of ninny who can't even finish a *chapter*, much less a *book.* . . .)

I'll actually be *happy* if you don't finish a chapter without stopping. That means you've felt the impact of what I've just said and want to stop and think about it for a while. Terrific.

Terrific.

So feel free to stop right *here* and think about what I just said. I just said, "You can undergo change, stand in the middle of it, and be okay. You can *very* okay."

That's a nice thought to gulp down. You can come back to the rest of this later. Whenever you choose. If ever. Heck, you may choose to just throw this book away. You get to decide.

That's the second good thing that's happened to you today. *You get to take control again.*

Yes, yes, it's a small thing—whether you're going to continue reading this book or not—but that's how it starts. That's how the rebuilding starts. . . .

So stop right now if you want to and give yourself some

Breathing Space

Breathe into what you've just read, then decide now if you want to go on, or rest with it for a while and meet with me here later . . . or not at all.

If you're ready to go on, drop down to . . .

WHAT YOU AND I ARE DOING HERE

If you have this book in your hand I'm assuming it's because the ground is shifting beneath you. Something is changing in your life—or already has changed—and it's something pretty important to you. It may even drive to the place of your personal safety or security. And you may be just beginning to confront the emotions that are coming up for you around all this. Or perhaps you've been facing those emotions for quite some time and can't seem to get past them.

Either that's the reason you were attracted to this book, or you bought it for someone else—a friend or a relative, a client or a member of your congregation . . . in which case, hurry and *finish it* and get it to that person immediately!

So now that we know what you're doing here, let me tell you what I'm doing here. I'm here because I *have* been where you are, and I want to help you. I'm here because something happened to me that helped me, and I want to pass it on.

I'm also here because I'm watching some pretty weird stuff going on in our world, the same stuff you're watching, and I see everything changing all over the place so fast that we can hardly keep track of it. I'm here because I know that unless we all find a way to deal with this *changing pace of change*—both collectively and individually—we're not going to be in a very good place. So I'm here to extend to you an invitation. An invitation in nine parts, to change the way you experience change forever. I'm here to see if I can engage you in "changing change."

Okay, so those are my reasons for being here. Now let's talk about what we might co-create here together. I was chatting about this with my wife, Em, and she said some things that really struck me. She said, "I am not seeing this book as a book. I am seeing it as a *commitment*. I see a person's picking it up as a commitment to opening to a whole new way of approaching life and of living each moment. This is like taking up a martial art, with the understanding that it will change the way you move through life. Or choosing to learn a foreign language until it is known so intimately that it one day feels like your natural way of speaking. These are lifelong pursuits that change your very *ground of being*.

"We live in an immediate-gratification society, where everything has to be delivered in fifteen minutes. But this isn't instant oatmeal. There are some really essential, important understandings that have been given to us through the ages and those can't be laid out in pamphlet form.

"This is a turning-yourself-inside-out so that you can be available to all of life again, so that you can actually feel alive *in* life again, which is what some of us haven't known since we were four years old—or maybe ever.

"The cover of this book says *When Everything Changes, Change Everything*. So I hope that people will sit down with this book, turn off their cellphone, and commit to at least a half hour at each reading and really *make it their practice.*"

I couldn't have said it better myself. I told her so.

"Well, nothing is more important than *how* you're experiencing life, honey," she smiled. "What else is there?" Then she brushed her dark hair to one side in the way that she has of stopping my heart, and I watched her face become very soft. "Nothing is more sacred to you than how you experience You, as an expression of life. *What else is there?*"

I agreed with her again. So now I invite *you* to take a look at how you've been experiencing and expressing life, and then ask that perfectly wonderful question that Dr. Phil has put into the global lexicon: *How has that been working for you?*

If it hasn't been working all that well, maybe you've brought yourself to the message here just in time. Maybe your soul has *led* you to this book so that, in Em's words, you can be available to all of life again.

(You know what? I think that's *exactly* what's happened. . . .)

Now what I'm going to do here is engage you on a personal level in a way that may be somewhat different from what you've encountered with other books. I don't want to talk *at* you, I want to talk *with* you.

I see you right in front of me now, and I see myself just talking with you quietly, hanging in there with you like a friend, walking through all that is happening to you these days, right alongside of you, and offering some gentle suggestions.

I know, I know . . . this is just a book, but it can be more than that if you'll let it be. Precisely because I *have* gone through much of what you're going through right now, I think we can create something together that could not only do what most books do—bring you information—but get to something very few books do: produce an actual, living, in-the-moment experience.

So I'm going to invite you to join me in eliminating the distance in time and space that exists between us. Now here's the remarkable thing about that. I don't even have to be alive for us to do this. *You* have to be, for sure, but I *don't*. I mean, you can't read the book if you are dead. But you *could* be reading this many years after *my* death . . . and we could still *con-*

nect at the level of Essence, through the shared experience of being human.

Remarkable when you think about it, isn't it? I'm right here, writing this, *now* . . . and *you're* right here, *reading* this now. Our *nows* don't have to coincide for our experience to. In this way, minds accordion Time.

So, whether I'm still alive when you read this or whether I've celebrated my Continuation Day, I'd like to co-create with you here an *interactive experience that can change your life.*

From experience I can tell you that the most important thing for you right now is to not allow yourself to be alone. I've been there in that aloneness, and I don't want you to ever have to be there. Ever. So this book is my way of being with you. This book is our *conversation.*

Do not pretend that The Longing
has not also lived in You,
swinging, like a pendulum.
You have been lost,
and thieved like a criminal
Your Heart
into the darkness.
But life is tired, Deep Friend,
of going on
without You.
It is like the hand of the mother
who has lost the child.
And if You are anything like me, You have been afraid.
And if You are anything like me,
You have known your own courage.
There is room in this boat:
take Your seat.
Take up Your paddle, and all of us
- *All of Us* -
shall row Our hearts
back
Home.

—'*The Longing*' © 2005 Em Claire

2.

THE FIRST CHANGE

Okay, so let's assume that my guess is right about why you're reading this book. If it is, you're going to be happy to know that there is a way to turn things around, and make of your life what you've always imagined it could be. There are many ways, actually, not just one. There are many paths to the mountaintop, and I want to be careful never to come off as the guy who thinks he has The Answer.

I do have *one* answer, though, and I know it's an answer, because it worked for me—and I've already *told* you what *I've* been through. So, here I am to tell you that one way to turn things around is to make . . .

NINE CHANGES THAT CAN CHANGE EVERYTHING

Now, in the conversation that follows I'm going to discuss these changes with you one by one. The changes will give you a way to deal with *calamity*, with tumultuous *shifts* in your reality, with the *collapse* of what you thought was going to be "so."

Should you choose to embrace the Nine Changes I am suggesting here, I believe you will be able to make even more changes in the way you move through life. Specifically, I believe you will be able to change Fear into Excitement, Worry into Wonder, Expectation into Anticipation, Resistance into Acceptance, Disappointment into Detachment, Enragement into Engagement, Addiction into Preference, Requirement into Contentment, Judgment into Observation, Sadness into Happiness, Thought into Presence, Reaction into Response, and a Time of Turmoil into a Time of Peace.

All of this seems almost too good to be true, I know. But it *is* true, and it *can* happen, and it can happen *in your life right now*.

Now I really *am* sounding like one of those

Rah!

Rah!

Ciss-boom-bah!

guys. So let me repeat: Facing change is not easy. Not without tools. Yet there *are* tools, and that's the good news. There is a way out of this forest. There is a light at the end of this tunnel. How fast you get over and get past what is happening right now depends on what path you take—and with whom you take it.

That gets me back to my first point—and the First Change. Let me say again that my experience has shown that in this it can be extremely beneficial to not go it alone here, but to have some support on this journey. That's why I'm here with you now. That's why I talking with you like this. If you'll stay with me here, you should be able to make it. So take all the "breathers" you want. Move through this exploration at your own pace. But whatever you do, *keep moving.* Don't let your mind get you stuck in some dark place.

Okay?

Now if you want to, this might be another good time to take some

Breathing Space

Breathe into the experience of what you've just read, then decide now if you want to go on, or rest with it for a while and meet with me here later.

When you're ready to go on, drop down to . . .

AN INVITATION TO STOP RECOILING

The first change you are invited to make is a change in the way you *deal* with change.

Most people recoil from change. They don't like it, because change is about stepping into unfamiliarity. It is about leaving something, or someone, behind and venturing forth into the Unknown. For some, it is about facing deep uncertainty, and even a threat to survival itself. And for many people, it is about doing this all alone.

This is the single biggest complaint I hear from people who have come to me through the years with sadness about the changes they're experiencing.

I've worked as a spiritual helper with more than 10,000 people, individually, through the years, and after talking with that many people for that many years I can tell you that you begin to hear and see the same things over and over again. And loneliness—emotional loneliness—*is what I saw the most.*

Now let me get back to my lady correspondent, Leah, who so kindly said I could use her e-mail messages in this book. As I mentioned before, Leah is going through some emotional turmoil right now. She wrote to my wife about it and I would like you to hear what she had to say.

(I should, perhaps, first explain what Em does in the world, so you understand why Leah even wrote to her. Em is a poet and uses her words as a balm from her medicine bag. She is finding as she presents her poetry in capitals around the world that it reflects the dramatic changes her life has undergone in the last five years—both the vistas and the valleys, the challenges and the breakthroughs. People have told her over and over again that after hearing her poetry their feeling is, "Oh, my God, I am not alone." They realize that she has experienced the same dismantling, and the same call to the re-creation of self in a new form, that they have. And so, many people have visited her website [www.EmClairePoet.com], and there, deeply touched and opened by her art, they connect with her.)

Here's what Leah shared with Em. . . .

"When I am feeling without hope and so very lost, I feel utterly alone. Yet I know that there are other people who hold this same dark sadness within them. When people are happy, they congregate and so share that energy. When we are in great pain, we cut ourselves off and the feeling of being isolated in the darkness and left out of life is so prevalent. Knowing I am not alone is so helpful to me, and maybe it will be helpful to someone else."

Leah's experience is not unusual. Her e-mail was just another in a fifteen-year string of evidence that demonstrated to me that self-isolation is just what we *do* when we feel the loss of something important to us through the changing of circumstances or conditions.

We shrink back into ourselves when the ground beneath us starts shifting. I've done it, haven't you? I don't do it anymore, but I have done it. That's why I recognize it so fast. Even people in committed relationships, even people in marriages or long-standing business partnerships, often turn quiet, reclusive, self-isolating (and sometimes, self-loathing).

So right now I'm hoping that you'll do everything in your power to make sure that you don't go through this critical time of your life by yourself. Reading this book is a good start. A great start, actually. But it's only the beginning.

So let's explore. . . .

CHANGE #1:
Change your decision to "go it alone"

This is a simple change, but it requires something from us that many people—I'm going to say, most people—are not used to, and not always comfortable with. It requires *transparency.*

The reason that so many of us tend to self-isolate when we are facing big problems—and by the way, have you noticed that almost every really big problem you've ever faced emerged from something that *changed?*—is that we have never given ourselves permission to be seen as less than perfect, or as someone who does not have it all together.

We've also been taught as children that we should not "burden others" with our problems. And finally, we've been told that most everything is our own fault anyway, so why would we go to someone else with it? It was made very clear: we made our bed and now we have to lie in it.

None of the above teachings have any value at all. The people who raised us were wrong about all of that. Every single bit of it.

The need to be "perfect" and to "have it all together" is a manifestation of a larger need: the need for approval.

Most of us learned as children that to get the approval of our parents and other elders around us, we needed to be good little boys and girls. Some of us were told about a person named Santa Claus who is "making a list, checking it twice, going to find out who's naughty and nice." And some of us were told about a God who loves us and watches over us . . . but will also judge us for everything we do "wrong" and will condemn us to everlasting damnation if that list is too long, or contains particular items.

So, we've poured love and fear into the same bowl and mixed them together pretty well. Our fear of losing love is what causes us to love ourselves with the same conditions with which others love us. It is easy, then, to be self-condeming and self-loathing. We've gotten so good at it that we'll do the work for others *even when they have no intention of doing it.*

This work of self-condemnation, self-recrimination, and self-disapproval must be done in private, of course, lest others disapprove of us for *this*. So we hide our emotions, and sometimes our very selves, from others when we are facing difficulties and problems.

The irony of this is that these are precisely the times when those who love us want to be there for us. Wouldn't you want to be there for someone you love who is hurting? Of course you would. It is, in fact, your first impulse.

What we have to do is trust that *it is the same with others*. People *want* to help us. They do *not* feel "burdened" by doing so. Quite the opposite. They feel uplifted.

Knowing that we've helped others brings us value, skyrockets our feelings of self-worth. Life suddenly begins to make sense. Or at least to give us, in that moment, a sense of higher purpose.

When you think about it, every occupation is nothing more than a way of helping others have something they want. Singers, dancers, painters, police officers, doctors, teachers, plumbers, actors, firefighters, stripteasers, priests, baseball players, photographers, flight attendants, waitresses, chairmen of the board . . . *everybody* is just doing something that helps someone else get something they want!

That's all we're doing here. We're not doing anything else. We're all just running around try to help somebody. Knowing this should make it easier to *accept* help—from a professional or from a loved one—when our own need is particularly acute. Why would we make it more difficult for someone to help us when help is exactly what we need, *and exactly what others want to give?*

So much for "don't burden others."

Okay? You got it? So much for *don't burden others. . . .*

So I'm going to invite you to make a commitment right now to reach out to another and share with that person how you're feeling about the changes that are occurring in your life. Tell them you're reading this book if you want to. You might even invite them to read it along with you.

I don't care whom you connect with, but connect with *somebody*. Connect with a relative. Connect with a friend. Connect with a professional counselor. Connect with a rabbi or an ulama or a priest or a minister. Connect with a member of the Changing Change Network. Connect with *somebody*. Because when you connect with somebody else, you connect with yourself.

I just said something very important there, and I don't want you to just skip over it. So please, let me say that again.

I said . . .

. . . *when you connect with somebody else, you connect with yourself.*

Talking with another person, communicating with a mind outside of your *own* mind, puts you in touch with the part of your Self that is bigger than your mind, larger than your thoughts. That's because the act of connecting with another pulls you out of your ongoing internal dialogue and into an external one.

In an external dialogue, another person can bring you fresh energy, provide a different perspective. They can come to the subject with a clear head, free of the self-judgment through which you are looking at everything. They see you as you really are, proving the irony that sometimes you have to get out of yourself to get into yourself. Sometimes you have to stop looking at yourself to see yourself.

To Love yourself, start here:

take your own hand—put it to your lips

then

lay the soft of your cheek, to the round of your shoulder

where

the faint musk

of the enduring dreams and the labors of your life

perfume you.

It's a start.

It's a beginning.

Now the ache of your heart

has a surface.

—'To Love Yourself' © 2006 Em Claire

3.

ONCE UPON A TIME . . .

IN ADDITION TO SEEKING dialogue with others, it is also very good to "go deep within" and re-companion with your own soul. *This is not the same as what you might have been doing lately.* This is an engagement with the soul, not with the mind.

What often happens when people are suddenly faced with really life-impacting change is that they *disconnect* from their soul by burrowing deep inside their *story.* Your story does not live in your soul, only in your mind.

Now, you would think that going deep within would produce ultimate clarity—and you would be right. In fact, my favorite axiom is: *If you don't go within, you go without.* Yet "going within" and "burrowing deep inside one's story" are two different things.

A story is a tale you tell yourself about yourself. It starts off, "Once upon a time . . . ," and it tells about everything that has happened to you, how and why. It is your internal narrative, a summary of the conclusions you have come to about your-self—conclusions that are rarely based on the truth about you and almost always include your harshest judgments about yourself.

Burrowing deep within *that* mess rarely produces clarity. In fact, I will say that it never does, because your story is not real. It exists only within your mind. It may seem very real to you, but it is not reality.

"Going within," on the other hand, is the taking of a jour-ney in which the Self *leaves* the mind and travels to the soul—where one's Personal Story does not exist. This allows you to come from a totally different space as you look at what is hap-pening to you. You go *to* a different space so that you can come *from* a different space.

This can be accomplished in many ways. In the end it's just about being quiet with yourself, but in a different way.

The irony is that you're *already* being quiet with yourself. You're probably in the midst of lots of self-reflection right now. But this is about exploring reflections that truly mirror who you are, rather than standing in front of one of those carnival house mirrors that make you look grotesque. Again, this is about being quiet with your soul, not with your mind.

Do not go to the mind for self-reflection! You'll lose track of yourself there. People lose touch with their own Best Self—or what I call their True Identity. (Yes, I'll explain that later.)

The biggest problem with "burrowing" in the mind is that not only do we confront our Personal (and not very flattering, as we tell it) Story, but we *add* to that story our own version of What Is Happening To Us Right Now, and why. This, too, we see reflected in that carnival mirror. Or, as Leah put it when I shared with her today how we all get caught up in our Personal Story. . . .

"For me, my story is intricately entwined with the external things happening in my life: having no income, being home-less, wondering how I will eat, being unable to find work. These circumstances 'inform' me about who I am—I draw conclusions about myself because of these external facts."

Indeed. So do we all. (Until we don't anymore.) When really big things change for the worse in our lives we often think it is our fault. It is something we did (or did not do) that caused it. We assume that we failed in some way. And in times of failure we recriminate against ourselves, we make ourselves wrong for everything we have done that "brought us to this," or everything we have failed to do, and we show very little mercy in that.

Or, if we don't go to self-blaming, we go to self-questioning. We burrow into our mind to figure out *why* what is going on is going on. When I was sharing about this book in a return e-mail with Leah she responded:

"What I want to know is, *why* do we do this? Why are these things happening? Why am I about to be homeless? Why am I unable to find work? Because I am _____? Because I did _____ and did not do _____?

"For me, personally, it would be helpful to understand why we, as humans, have this need to know the WHY of what is happening to us. It must be some fundamental, basic need to make sense of things around us—?

"Or maybe I need to better know here how to separate that from the external circumstances of my current situation: having no money and no immediate way to 'fix things'—because those external things are very real right now."

Either way—whether we fault ourselves for being the cause of our unwelcome change, or fault ourselves for not knowing what the cause *is*—we can't imagine how anyone could love us (we think they must be "just saying that") because we can't imagine loving ourselves, and we get lost in our own minds. We lose track of our True Selves, of our Best Selves, as we wander around inside our now-expanded story. Was there ever a worse person? A bigger failure? A more unable, unreliable, undesirable, worthless human being?

What's funny is that *we know that we are doing this.* We can feel ourselves condemning ourselves—and so then we condemn ourselves for doing *that.* This pushes us even further away from our True Selves. And if others who know us well ask what's going on with us, we say, "Oh, nothing. I'm just not myself today."

Nothing could be closer to the truth.

And, as I said, we know it. Deep down inside we know this is not Who We Really Are—but we don't know how to get *back* to that; we don't know what to *do* about it.

So we head for the mind and go back to the inner chatter. We keep talking to ourselves about what's going on. The only problem is, we can't *reach* our selves—not our True Selves, not our Best Selves—because our *story* is blocking the way. We begin thinking we *are* that story, that *this* is the truth about us, and that everything *else* is The Show.

For us now, there's The Show and there's The Story. We convince ourselves that all the Good Stuff is part of The Show that we're "putting on," while the Bad Stuff is the Real Stuff. That's the Real Story on us.

Any of this sound familiar? It does to me, because I've done every one of these things. And still do some of this today . . . until I pull myself out of it. This book is about *how I do that.*

So if you're "not feeling yourself today," I'm going to suggest that you take Suggestion #1 and change your decision to "go it alone."

Make this change today.

Not tomorrow.

Today.

Decide to connect with your soul, and then decide to *reach out.* Find someone who does not operate inside your story. Someone who knows you well and does not see you as you think you are, but as you really are. Have a conversation with *that* person and you may find that this one change alone has changed a great deal about how you experience the change that is now changing your life.

If you *have* no one else in your life right now who can bring you this opportunity for external dialogue, I have a little surprise for you. I'm going to make this a *two-way book.* I'm going to invite *you* to talk with *me,* and with others who have already read this book, *even as you make your way through this material.*

I'm saying that you can put the book down and connect with someone *right now.* Someone who knows what you're going through. Someone who's been there. Is that a terrific idea, or what? It might even be a revolutionary way to experience a book.

Perhaps you just want to connect with someone because you have a question about something you've read here, or want a fuller explanation, or want to know how others have experienced what's being discussed. Fair enough. Just get online and head to the special website that has been set up just for you, to help you change the way change is being experienced in your life. Just go to . . .

www.ChangingChange.net

Now get *this* . . . you can not only write to us and receive an answer, you can even *talk* with us, in real-time conversations via regularly scheduled group conference calls and teleclasses. You can explore with the network what you're experiencing and reading *even as you're reading and experiencing it,* and ask network members any question that you wish.

At this same website you can watch videos of others who have moved through great change in their lives, as they answer questions and discuss how they did it.

And it *need not end there.* You can also receive *private life coaching* from certain members of the Network, attend one-day Changing Everything workshops that I present, and even participate in the extended long-form spiritual renewal retreats that I facilitate.

The point: You can have as much help as you want. The important thing is for you not to feel alone. There's no need for you to handle what's happening to you right now all by yourself. There are others who can assist you. People who care. I'm one of them. And there are more. Teammates who have joined the Changing Change community and who have created the

Network. Folks who will gently and lovingly walk you through what's happening right now and bring you out on the other side.

So . . . if it feels good to do so, get right to a computer, go to www.ChangingChange.net and post an entry there. Someone who is going through, or has gone through, exactly what you are going through right now will send you a reply before too long. Please, don't be too closed off, or timid, or embarrassed, or stubborn, or *whatever*, to share about your situation with another.

Connect. *Connect.* CONNECT.

If nothing else . . . if absolutely nothing else . . . *keep reading this book.* You're connecting here with *me*, and I'm connecting with you.

And that's great.

So, would you like to move on?

It's a beautiful time to be alive.
And the long walk home is peopled—
We, are *everywhere*.
Yet the struggle to surrender is where we walk alone.
So the next time you fall
look
to either side where you lie
and take the hand
of your dear Sister or Brother
whose own face is muddied.
We can rise together,
even if we fall alone—
for it's a beautiful time to be alive
even
on this long walk home.

—*'Rise Together'* © 2007 Em Claire

4

THE NORMAL RESPONSE TO CHANGE

UM . . . WELL . . . hold it just a bit. I need to warn you about something.

I say things more than once.

Please don't go crazy as our conversation proceeds, thinking, "Didn't he just say that before?" I probably *did* just say it before.

At the advertising agencies in New York they claim that the average person does not totally absorb the total content of any message until it's heard five or six times. I don't know if that's true, but I do know that I, myself, rarely pick up the whole message about anything—much less its nuance and its real impact—the first time I hear it. So I just wanted to tell you that I'm going to be saying some things a couple of times here. Maybe three times. Heck, maybe even four.

I'll try to make my restatements interesting . . . but I'm going to ask you to have some patience with me around this;

to indulge me a little. This book is written in a circular fashion, not in a straight line. That's the style I've chosen here because I want to be sure that I'm being as clear as I can be about all that I want to share, and sometimes repetition helps me to feel assured about that. Okay?

Now . . . as I said earlier, I don't know what has changed in your life, but I do know that the change has been disruptive. That much I'm sure of. Why? Because *all* change is disruptive, even change for the better.

So don't be too upset with yourself if this situation is "really getting to you." It's very normal that it would. In fact, very often change can create more than disruption. It can bring up a lot of emotions. How you experience change—as a time of turmoil and distress or a time of peace and creativity—depends on what emotions you move through.

Nearly all change produces fear. Did you know that? I mean, not only the "bad" kinds of change, but even change for the *better.*

You decide to get married—and immediately move into fear. What if the love doesn't last? What if you chose the wrong partner?

You take a new and much better job—and immediately move into fear. What if you can't do what you said you could do when you applied? What if it doesn't work out?

You rearrange the furniture in your living room—and immediately move into fear. What if your partner doesn't like it when he or she comes home? Maybe you should put it all back the way it was and talk about it first . . .

Some people can't even change their *hairstyle* without moving into fear. What if this looks silly? Will I lose what little I had going for me?

It's crazy, but this is how we think. We do this. You do it and I do it. All of us do this kind of stuff. Because Sameness is comfort. Even Sameness that's killing us, even Sameness that's boring us to tears. Yet someone once said: Life begins at the end of your Comfort Zone. That's a good thing to remember. *Life begins at the end of your Comfort Zone.*

So if you're feeling uncomfortable right now, know that the change taking place in your life is a *beginning*, not an ending.

All right, it's an ending. Let's not kid ourselves. Something important has ended. Something meaningful has stopped. Something that was very present in your life has disappeared, vanished, evaporated, *just like that*. Maybe it's a person. Maybe it's a dream.

Maybe it's the end of your safety, of your security. Maybe we're talking about more here than the loss of a boyfriend, or changing jobs. Maybe what's happening in your life right now is much more threatening than that.

Okay, so let's call it what it is. Let's not try to fool around here. You know what's going on in your life, so let's say it like it is. But, having said that, here's what *I* want to say . . .

What*ever* has just ended . . . it's also a beginning.

Now remember, you're hearing from a guy who spent a year on the street. You're talking to someone who lost everything. Job. Wife. Family. Every possession he ever had or held dear. Even my *car* was stolen. Right off the streets of Portland, Oregon, in the middle of the night. I already had no home. I was "camping out" for a while in the apartment of a friend until I could get myself re-situated . . . when I went outside one morning to find my old, beaten up Chevy Impala gone.

Gone.

The *last* of my personal possessions was in that car. Now I had nothing. *Nothing.* I had the clothes on my back. A few shaving things and stuff that I had taken into the apartment. I mean, that was *it.*

So I know about endings. And I have seen what I absolutely thought and felt was the end of *everything* turn into the beginning of a life of which I could only have dreamed. So I feel I've earned the credentials to at least plant that seed in your own thinking. Maybe it's too early—maybe way too early—to talk in terms of getting on with new beginnings, and maybe the conditions of your life won't even allow that right now, but it's not too early to at least plant a seed. We've all heard it a hundred times, and it seems incredibly trite to say it again, now, but . . . here we go anyway. . . .

"For every door that closes there's another one that opens."

I don't care *what* you've lost—your job, your house, your spouse, your credit, your dream, your hopes, even your health . . . I don't care *what* you've lost or *what* has so drastically changed, *you can start your life all over again, and achieve even greater heights.*

I promise you.

That has proven to be true so many times in my life that I have ceased to become upset when things are changing. I just look to see what's next. The idea of something different intrigues me now. It no longer scares me.

Even scary things no longer scare me. Like losing virtually my entire retirement account during the financial meltdown of the Fall of '08. People were running around going, "Oh, my! Oh, my!" and my only thought was, "Easy come, easy go. It's all perfect. Life will go on. I've been on the street once, I can do it again."

I have to admit, when you've lived outside for a year your point of view gets changed. But a person doesn't have to experience such an extreme in order to bring wisdom forward. It's there, back there, in the subconscious of all of us. We all know all we need to know—and we all *know* that we know it. Some of us just don't believe it. It's "too good to be true," so we don't believe it.

My "belief" has turned to "knowing." I've lived long enough to know that most of the things I worried about never happened, that most of the things I felt bad about turned out to be for the better, and that most of the things I hoped would stay the same couldn't stay the same if they wanted to, because change is the Process of Life Itself.

I touched on this earlier. Let me reiterate it here. Life *is* change, and when there is nothing that is changing, there is nothing that is living. Everything that lives, moves. And that means everything that *is*. Even a rock moves. Put a microscope to a rock. Peer inside its molecular structure. You will find a small universe down there, displaying an interesting characteristic: *everything is moving.*

Life is movement. Movement is change. Every time a submolecular particle swings through time and space, something is changing. Change, therefore, is inevitable. It is the nature of life itself.

The trick in life is not to try to avoid change, but to *create* change. (That's what part 2 of this book is all about.) Then it is the kind of change you choose. But right now, you're in the middle of a moment of great change in your life that you did *not* create (not consciously, anyway), and you're dealing with your emotions around that. Those emotions include fear, most likely, at some level. And sadness, perhaps. And maybe even a little anger. Hell, maybe a *lot* of anger.

I have to believe you're dealing with at least one of these three. So let's explore this. Let's look more closely at fear.

You want to have a little break first? Okay, if you need a good place to put the book down for now, this would be it. Give yourself a little

Breathing Space

Breathe into what you've just read, then decide now if you want to go on, or rest with it for a while and meet with me here later.

If you're ready to go on, drop down to . . .

NOTICING THAT YOU'RE PERFECTLY NORMAL

Nice. Way to take care of yourself. Looking at what you're doing—stopping and just *looking at what you're doing*—then actively deciding what you want to do next, is a wonderful way to take care of yourself. You've done that just now, and that's great. That's a good habit to get into.

Okay, so we're talking about fear.

Fear is ubiquitous—and understandable. What we're afraid of, after all, is the unknown. That's the biggest fear that most of us face. Fear of the unknown. And most change throws us into the path of the unknown. Not all change, but most of it.

Some change takes us to a place to which we've been before—and *that's* what we fear. But most change is not that predictable. Most change leaves us in the Space of Unknowing what will be. And so, we walk with apprehension. (That's just a softer word for fear.)

Sometimes what change brings us is the fear that we will never get to where we wanted to go; that life will continue to do nothing but take away our hopes and our dreams, rob us of our opportunities, kill our spirit, and strip us of raison d'être.

All of this is normal. It's understandable that you would feel that way. After all, life *has* done some of these things. And always the damage has come in the form of something that has changed.

So it's good to be aware that a certain amount of fear is going to accompany *every* change in your life—a change for the worse or a change for the better. Knowing this can stop you from moving into fear about *change itself.* If you start fearing change *generically* you could wind up shrinking from ever making any kind of change at all for the rest of your days—even a change that obviously *should* be made for your own good.

You're not going to stop change from happening simply by not making any changes yourself. All you'll do is stop change from happening the way *you* want it to happen. The world on this very day is evidence of that.

As is the case with Us,
I make, and You break asunder
whatever comfort I had
constructed.
Never certain
what You want from Me;
believing all I am told
about how it is that
Life is supposed to be Our Unfolding Joy
I cower, sometimes
God
in the corner, like an animal
who doesn't understand the thunder;
who doesn't understand the lightning.

Who doesn't understand, *Enlightening*.

—'I Cower' © 2007 Em Claire

5.

IT'S JUMP TIME

IT MAY BE HELPFUL to know that what's going on with you in your personal life is going on all over, in the collective life on this planet. That may make you feel a little bit less "picked on" by the universe—and therefore a little bit less isolated.

Right now so much is changing for so many people. The world's economies are undergoing radical alterations, causing all of humanity to realign its basic life priorities. The world's politics have changed, and we are seeing things we never thought we'd see. The world's medicine and science and technology are uncovering amazing secrets that are shifting our understanding of the very basics of life itself. The world's newest thoughts about relationship and marriage have moved many people beyond their comfort zone. And the way so many people are handling conflict today has brought sheer terror into our lives.

On a personal level, people are losing their jobs, their savings, even their homes. As a larger and larger segment of the population grows older and older, more of us are watching family members make the transition we call death. Marriages and partnerships are ending more frequently, and over far less, than ever before. Between these last two developments, we are losing loved ones from our lives at a frantic pace. Our approaches to parenting and to education are shifting so dramatically that they are impacting the dynamics of interior family relationships in ways of which we could not have dreamt just a short time ago.

All of this is part of a larger process now going on in the world. The whole of human society is in the throes of reinventing itself. Yet most of us are doing it without a diagram, without a road map, without any tools. That's why what I'm sharing with you here can be so helpful.

The point of my telling you all of this is not to depress you even more, but to help you get clear that *this is not something that is just happening to you.* The good news is that there is a way to grab the reins of this runaway stagecoach, at least on a personal level. There is a way to control and alter your reaction to change—and, going on from there, to control, direct, and create the changes themselves.

I've been setting the stage now for a bit, because I want you to have a context—a really rich context—within which to hold all that we're going to be looking at presently.

We are moving through what anthropologist and social scientist Jean Houston calls Jump Time in her remarkable book by that title. Jump Time, Jean says, is a moment in the eternal cycle of life when we monumentally shift every aspect of our experience, much as humanity did during the 300 years of the Renaissance (a blink of an eye on the clock of eternity), when everything from art to politics to culture to governance to commerce to education to religion to human sexual experience to partnerships and parenting to how to eat, drink, and *talk*, for heaven's sake, changed so fundamentally that nothing—literally *nothing*—was ever the same again.

The heart-stopping characteristic of this, our new Renaissance, is that it is not taking place over 300 years, but thirty. Yes, I said *thirty years.* This owes to that breathtaking tenfold increase in the width, breadth, scope, and speed of global intercultural communication that I spoke of earlier.

We are already living on the edge of what I call *The Time of Instaparency*, when everything is instantly known, transparently. Such moment-to-moment awareness of all that's going on everywhere produces alterations in perspective that start dominoes falling all over the place.

Humanity is not going to be able to deal with this—*you're* not going to be able to deal with this—unless The Answer to Everything is revealed. That's what we're going to do here. We're going to unlock the secret. You and me. Right here, in Chapter Sixteen.

No, no, don't jump ahead to that chapter now! We need to talk first about why the changes in your life have been so painful. Then I'll share with you that truly astonishing truth, so that change never has to be painful again. Not even calamitous change—like losing everything; like being out on the street. Yet unless you have the foundation that we're laying here, the secret itself will seem hollow, shallow.

So let's rest here for a bit, if it feels good to do so, and contemplate the speed with which you and your world are encountering change. Just . . . breathe in and

Relax for a moment

Be right here, right now. Thinking about all that's been said, try not to "do anything" with it. Just "be" with it, breathe into it, and be grateful for this moment. Then . . .

. . . when you're ready to go on, drop down to . . .

EVENTS VS. REALITY . . .
WHAT DOES IT ALL MEAN?

Look, I know that I've placed before myself a big task. I'm hoping to convince you that the changes in your life right now do not have to be painful, and I'm clear that your life so far has demonstrated to you that change *is* painful. Yet the key to ending the pain is knowing what *causes* the pain, what *causes* the hurt. The key is knowing *why* you feel the way you feel.

And here's the news about *that*. . . .

It is not the change itself. It's not the losing of the job or the end of the relationship or the sudden inability to pay the bills or whatever else is occurring in your outside world. It is how you are thinking about it.

This is the same thing that causes sadness. This is the same thing that causes anger. It is never an exterior event, it is always an interior process. An event and your reality *about* that event are not the same thing.

Oh-oh, here we go again. That's important enough to say twice.

An event and your reality about that event are not the same thing.

An event is one thing; your reality of it is another. Events are created by conditions and occurrences outside you. Reality is created by conditions and occurrences *inside* you—in your mind. It is here that *events* are turned into *data,* which are turned into *truths,* which are turned into *thoughts,* which are turned into *emotions,* which are turned into *experiences,* which form your *reality.*

Now if we could just *change* one of those. . . .

We are Lightbabies.
Golden Grace.
Wings, meant to Fly.
We are delicate, and pregnant
with goodness.
We are each made of such a quiet
that the entire Universe
can hear us.

There is only the unfolding, the opening
ever happening.
All else are thoughts—
lollipops for the mind.
We, are *Lightbabies*
parading
as Humankind.

—*'Lightbabies'* © 2007 Em Claire

6.

THE SECOND CHANGE

THERE ARE SIX THINGS that create your reality in this physical experience that we call life. I just named them a moment ago. They are, again: Events, Data, Truths, Thoughts, Emotions, and Experience. If any of these six elements change, your reality will change. That means that if you want your current experience of the current change in your life to change, you have to change one of the elements. All of which brings us to . . .

CHANGE #2:
Change your choice of emotions

What I want to tell you is that you can *change your choice of emotions*—and thus, change how you're experiencing change itself. I can't tell you all about how you can do that in this one chapter, because there's more to it than I can put in a few lines here. And it's all intrinsically tied in with Changes 3 and 4—so we really have to consider all three together. But for now, let me just say that you can change your emotions about anything. About what's happening in your life right now, about yourself, about this book.

About anything.

Now you may not think this it is possible. You may even feel that it is bordering on smugness or arrogance for me to so much as suggest it. I also know that you've heard all this before, in "self-help" books, in lectures . . . so you may be thinking, listen, if it's all that simple, why can't the average person just *do it?* Isn't it cruel to hold it out there like a carrot, when you know it's on a stick and most people can't get to it?

Yes, if that were the case, it would be cruel. But I would never do that. I would never put something in front of you that it is utterly impossible for you to reach. I'm not trying to make you crazy, I'm trying to make you happy.

So, even though you've heard some of this before, this time I'd like you to really think about it. No, really. I mean, please, just close your eyes and think about this. *Because what I've said here is one of the most important (and revolutionary) things anyone will ever say to you.* And even if you *have* heard it before, you may not have deeply explored the possibility of its being true. So, will you do that now?

I mean, is it possible that this is something you simply do not completely understand . . . the understanding of which could change everything?

This time I'm *asking* you to stop reading. Just for a second. Just for a brief pause. Just time enough to decide how you want to feel about this.

Did you catch the irony there? I want you to *choose* how you wish to feel about the idea that you can choose how you wish to feel.

So please go ahead. Close the book and think about it. Ask yourself some questions. What would my life be like if I thought I could actually *select* my emotions, rather than be subjected to them? Is it possible to change an emotion after I'm already having it? Not ignore it or operate "on top of it," but actually, really and truly *change the emotion I'm having.* Can I do that? At will?

Please ponder that question—and what it would mean if the answer were yes—and take some . . .

Breathing Space

Breathe into what you've just read, then . . . decide now if you want to go on, or rest with it for a while and meet with me here later . . . or not at all.

If you're ready to go on, drop down to . . .

THE SPONSOR OF ALL EMOTIONS

Okay, so we're talking here about emotions. Well, *I'm* talking about emotions. Meanwhile, you're having them. All that you're trying to do is deal with the changes that are occurring in your life, with the very threatening calamities that may be happening, while I'm launching into a small lecture on human psychology and what causes emotions and how we can change them.

But you know what? I wouldn't dare do such a thing, I wouldn't even bring any of this up, if I didn't think it was going to help you. *Right here, right now.* No matter *what's* going on. Yes, even if you've lost your job. Even if you've lost your house. Even if you feel you are in danger of losing everything.

As I've said, I think I know a little about what you're going through. I've been there. And it took me years to figure out what I'm going to be telling you now. I just didn't get it. I just didn't understand. Until I did. (With a little help from a Friend. . . .)

So now, let me double back just a bit and reinforce the point I just made about emotions. And I promise you, you'll see how this all ties together and how this relates directly to you . . . as well as how it can make a real difference in this moment of your life. I mean, that's the idea here, yes? That's the point of us having this conversation, right? Otherwise I'm just flapping my gums here.

So . . . let's dive back in. Let's look at that one specific emotion of fear (I use this one because it is so powerful) and see how we can change that.

Fear is an emotion that you have that is sponsored by a thought that you have, which produces an experience that you have of an event that has occurred in your life. Most people think that fear is produced directly by the *event*. That is, most people think that the sequence is: event=experience. This is not true. The proof that it's not true is that emotion does not arise uniformly. The same things do not produce fear, for example, in two different people. They sometimes do, but they just as often do not.

A roaring lion can produce fear in one person and not in another (say, a lion tamer). Heights can produce fear in one person and not in another (say, the star of a high-wire act). Giving a speech can produce fear in one person (it has been listed in survey after survey as among the single biggest fears faced by many human beings) and not in another (say, a lecturer or an entertainer).

So we can agree that no two people can be guaranteed to have the same experience (fear) when faced with the same exterior event, yes? Heck, the same event does not even produce the identical experience in the *same* person every time.

So what *does* produce the fear? If it is not the roaring lion or the height of the ladder or the audience waiting to hear you, then what is it?

It's something *inside* you. It's your ideas and your memories and your projections and your concepts and your apprehensions and your understandings and your desires and your conditioning and more. And all of these things fall into one broad category.

Thoughts.

It is your *thoughts* that sponsor your fears, and nothing else. Thoughts sponsor *all* emotions.

Now this is both a revolutionary and controversial statement that I am making here, because standard brain science says that is it just the other way around. Neuroscientists tell us that emotion comes *before* thought, as a product of the brain's limbic system, and that "thought" occurs in the higher regions of the brain, which analyze the emotions we are having. I am saying here that the opposite is true. I am saying that the limbic system produces what I call a Truth (an overall mental *concept* of something), from which emerges a Thought, which generates an Emotion.

Every time you display *any* kind of emotion you can say, "And now, a word from our sponsor!" Like the sponsors on television, thoughts stop the show.

That fact that thoughts sponsor emotions is the greatest news you could ever hear.

If we accept the view of scientists that it is the other way around, we accept as a matter of fact that each of us has a built-in handicap: an utter inability to decide objectively which emotions we are going to feel. We accept that *we are subject to our emotional reactions* and then have to *overcome them* with our thoughts if we want them to be different.

My thesis here is that it is not a question of overcoming our emotions to get them to be what we want them to be, but of creating them that way *from the start*. This idea may be new to medical science, but it is not new to spirituality, which insists that we are more than biological machines, and that the Mind is not the same as the brain, but is far more complex and sophisticated—and that the Soul is even *bigger* and more sophisticated than the Mind!

In this moment, as you face all the changes that are occurring in your life, this is the best news you could ever receive. Why? Because it gives you tools you never thought you had. Because it reverses the standard medical model, putting thoughts *before* emotions, rather than after them—meaning that we are in charge here, since *thoughts are changeable*.

Just a while ago we talked about changing your emotions. I said that changing emotions was the way to change Change Itself. I'm now going to tell you *how* you can change emotions. *Change your thoughts.*

Whereas the Heart is used to being
the only place where Love is found
a Mind full of joy
draws the Heart like a moth,
into a surprisingly *different* flame.
A flame where nothing burns—
no wings are forfeited.
As if God stretches the length of The Home
to abide in every room at once,

simply

because

We

can

*

—*'A Mind Full of Joy'* © 2007 Em Claire

7.

THE THIRD CHANGE

You MAY NOT BE able to change the fact that things are changing, but you *can* change your *thought* about the things that are changing.

Not only is this possible, it is next on the list of Nine Changes That Can Change Everything.

CHANGE #3:
Change your choice of thoughts

Thought is an idea that you are *making up*. The change that is occurring in your life is not something you are making up, but your thought about it is. That thought often bears no relationship to ultimate reality, it often bears no relationship to observed reality, yet it often does bear a relationship to distorted reality. In fact, it often *creates* it.

Oh-oh, this is Something Big here. I'm thinking we should not just fly right past what was just said. Let's look at it more closely. What I said was . . .

"Your thought is something you are *making up*. It often bears no relationship to ultimate reality, it often bears no relationship to observed reality, yet it often does bear a relationship to distorted reality. In fact, it often *creates* it."

Now, I just introduced a whole new idea there. Did you catch me at it? I just referred to three different "realities" . . .

Ultimate Reality
Observed Reality
Distorted Reality

I have come to call this the Triune Reality—three versions of reality existing at one time.

There is Ultimate Reality (what is "so" about what is going on, what is "so" about *why* it is going on, and what is "so" about *you*), there is Observed Reality (what is readily apparent right in front of you), and there is Distorted Reality (what you imagine is going on).

Which one of these realities you experience in any given moment is up to you. It depends on what your mind entertains *prior to forming a thought*.

The sweet Unveiling is so becoming
there is perhaps nothing
more beautiful.

The *glide* that you once called
"walking."

Your fears
dropped as gently as lingerie.

As Who You Are
naked child
turns every purpose
Lightward
toward what has always been
right
here
shining
as

You.

—*'The Sweet Unveiling'* © 2006 Em Claire

8.

THE FOURTH CHANGE

WE'RE MOVING VERY FAST now, and I don't want you to think that you're hearing all I have to say about these changes. There is *much* more to say, in fact. I'm just introducing Changes #2, #3, and #4 right now, to give you an idea of where we're headed in this conversation. This is going to be quite a ride, and I want you to have a sense of the terrain.

Really, these three changes are interlinked and, as I said a moment ago, they should be considered together. So the exploration here is going to be rather free-flowing, as a chat between friends would be, as opposed to following an outline and being more structured, as a lecture might be. I trust that you'll see the close interlinking between Change #2, Change #3, and Change #4 as we go.

So here, as we lay down the road map, is . . .

CHANGE #4:
Change your choice of truths

Earlier I said that the events of your life are created by conditions and occurrences outside you, but that reality is created by conditions and occurrences *inside* you—in your mind. It is there, I said, that *events* are turned into *data,* which are turned into *truths*, which are turned into *thoughts,* which are turned into *emotions*, which are turned into *experiences,* which form your *reality.*

Now let me put those elements in a straight line, with *plus* and *equal* signs placed strategically between them, so that you can have a way to visualize this. This allows us to focus in on the process of reality-creation a little more sharply.

As I observe it, that process works like this . . .

event + data + truth + thought + emotion = experience = reality

I call this the Line of Causality, and I'll be bringing it into our discussion again. This is the path the mind travels on its way to producing your reality.

You'll notice that on this line, Emotion comes before Experience, and produces it. Thought, likewise, comes before Emotion, and gives birth to *it*. Truth comes before Thought, and gives birth to *that*. And we'll get to the "Data" part later.

What the line does not show is that there are three *kinds* of truth. This is more than a little important to know, because it is the existence of these three kinds of truth that leads to the possibility of a Triune Reality. Put another way, if there were only one kind of truth, there would be but a single reality.

The three kinds of truth are . . .

The Actual Truth
The Apparent Truth
The Imagined Truth

In a bit I'm going to explain all of this, and I think you'll find it fascinating. These are what I have called the Mechanics of the Mind. For right now, know that it's really as simple as A-B-C. Each step away from "A" takes you farther from peace.

If peace is what you are searching for during this moment of change and turmoil in your life, if peace is that for which you yearn, you will want to journey upward from Imagined Truth to Apparent Truth to Actual Truth, so that you may shift your basis from Distorted Reality to Observed Reality to Ultimate Reality.

This is what personal and global transformation is all about. This is what every human whom we have honored with the name of Master has done. And this is what you can do right here, right now, on this day.

In your life, has everything changed? Then *change every-thing.* Start rearranging your thinking about "reality." Reality is not static, it is fluid.

(Well, that's not exactly accurate. It IS static, but our *experience* of it changes. And that, of course, is what this whole book is about. The exploration here is about how to change your experience of Change Itself. Or, put another way, how to change your experience of reality—since Change is the *constant* reality.)

I have to tell you, I felt like I'd been awakened out of a sound sleep when I first "got" that there are three levels of reality, and that we can experience the things that are happening in our lives at the level of Distortion, the level of Observation, or the level of Ultimate Truth. It took me a long time to figure this out. It took me a long time to notice what I am telling you here so casually.

I don't want it to take you as long as it took me. I want you to be able to grasp this now. First as an intellectual concept, *then as a functional tool.* You need this tool now, not ten years from now, not ten months from now, not ten weeks from now. Not even ten *days* from now. You need this tool in your hands now, because now is when you're moving through incredible changes.

If someone had told me this stuff in the moment that I was going through big changes . . . what a difference that would have made. So here goes. Let me tell you *all* of what I've uncovered about this.

Each of these "realities" that I've just spoken of is remarkably different from the others—not a little bit different, *remarkably* different—and the differences between them arise out of those three brands of truth that I referred to earlier.

One of the biggest surprises of my life was learning that there is no such thing as absolute truth.

Now that should be on a billboard somewhere. Heck, everywhere. On every road and highway there should be a huge sign:

THERE IS NO SUCH THING AS ABSOLUTE TRUTH

Ever caught yourself asking someone, "Are you actually *buying* that?" Well, this is about that. This is about what you "buy into" every day.

When you go into the Supermarket of Life you'll find Truth packaged in three brands. You can buy Actual Truth, you can buy Apparent Truth, or you can buy Imagined Truth.

For right now we're going to pretend that Actual Truth is not on the shelf. I don't want to discuss the *actuality* of things just yet. (That's what part 2 of this book is about.) I just want to look at Apparent Truth (what we have *observed*) and Imagined Truth (what we have *distorted*). Only when we see these clearly can we understand Actual Truth.

The Apparent Truth is based on what you have observed in the past to be happening when you saw something similar to what you see in front of you right now. It is what you think is apparently so, based on your history, about the physical event that is occurring in the present moment.

Your relationship has ended. Or you got laid off. Or you lost your home. Or someone close to you has passed on. Or you've become an empty nester, with your children suddenly no longer in your home after being a huge part of your life for twenty years. Or whatever.

This is what's going on right now in your physical world. It's what's happened. You know it happened because it is your direct observation. If you stay in your Apparent Truth, you will be okay, because your Apparent Truth will give you all the facts of a similar experience you have had in your past. But will you stay there? I mean in your thoughts, will you stay there? Or will you run to your Imagined Truth? And, if you embrace your Imagined Truth rather than the Apparent Truth, will you have the tools with which to return *to* the Apparent Truth?

I believe the Nine Changes That Can Change Everything could be those tools. Read on and see if you agree.

I left The Home so long ago now
that I would not recognize my own face.
I constructed the Boat of My Life
and I set out
into the open sea
waving to all who knew
that the seas would give me
everything I could handle
and everything I could not
and yet they waved, and I set out
into the open sea
in the Boat of My Life:
built from Soul, crafted by Heart
and with great innocence I pushed off
into the open sea
and have been away from my Home
so long now that I would not recognize my own face
but I know that Home—
Home
remembers me

—*'Long at Sea'* © 2007 Em Claire

9.

THERE IS ONLY ONE EMOTION

So, HERE YOU ARE in the present moment, facing the changes that you're dealing with right now, and there is no doubt that you are having some emotion around that. Strong emotion, perhaps. Emotion you may be having a hard time dealing with.

It is this emotion that is producing your Here-and-Now experience. It is this experience that you call your reality.

Why are you having all this emotion? Why are you so angry, or so frightened, or so sad? Mostly because you, like most people, do not come from your Apparent Truth when forming your thoughts about a present-day event. If you did, things would be a lot easier. But most people come from their Imagined Truth about what's happening in their present moment. This is what most people buy into.

A lion appears out of nowhere and roars. You experience being petrified—because you imagine that you are in danger of being mauled. A mountain road takes a turn and you find yourself driving on the outside ledge, with a 3,000-foot drop-off just outside the window. You experience being terrified—because you imagine that with one wrong move you could die. An audience is awaiting your entrance for a major speech. You experience being paralyzed—because you imagine that you stand a good chance of going out there and disappointing everybody while making a fool of yourself.

A spouse abruptly leaves. Or you get laid off from your job. Or you lose your home. You experience being stunned, angry, mortified. And, sooner or later . . . afraid.

All of this is based on your Imagined Truth, which is that this is "bad," that you're going to be "unhappy," that lots of "struggle" lies ahead, or whatever.

It's okay to feel this fear, of course. In the face of the change that you're moving through, it's to be expected. It's nothing to be ashamed of. It's very normal. It's how we've been raised. We've been told that fear exists, that fear is real.

The Actual Truth is that there is *no such thing as fear*. In fact, there is no such thing as *any* emotion, other than one. All the other expressions are repackagings. There is only one emotion, one energy, in the universe: the energy, the emotion, that we call Love. When you know this, everything changes.

Now I know all this may sound a bit "airy-fairy" or "new agey" to you, but when you know *why* there is nothing but Love, everything will become clear and your life will feel—can I use this word?—healed. Remember, experience is produced by emotion, so understanding that everything is a demonstration of the emotion called Love can alter your entire experience of life.

But how can *change* be a demonstration of Love? Didn't we just say, haven't we been saying for quite a while now, that *fear* is the emotion most people feel surrounding change—even change for the better? Am I seriously suggesting now that fear does not exist?

Yes, I am. That's exactly what I'm saying. Because (and here comes a wonderful revelation) . . . *fear is a demonstration of Love.*

If you did not love yourself, you would not fear for yourself, you would not be afraid of anything, because you would not care what happened to you. You would not even care if you survived. The "survival instinct" is nature's way of expressing love.

If you did not love another, you would not fear for another, or be afraid of what might happen to that other, because you would not *care* what happened.

Simple, isn't it? And so we see with impeccable logic that Fear and Love are the same thing, expressed differently. Likewise, every other emotion is love in another form. There is only one emotion. That emotion is Love, expressed in a thousand different ways. It is the Actual Truth. When we talk more about that Actual Truth a bit later, this whole concept will come together more fully. Then you will see a quantum leap in your ability to deal with all change peacefully.

But for now let's do as I suggested. Let's look at two of the Three Brands of Truth: Apparent Truth and Imagined Truth. It's important that we do, because *this is the key to everything.*

So . . . as I was saying . . .

. . . most people live in their Imagined Truth when things change, having been held down there by their past. This Imagined Truth births a thought, out of which arises an emotion, which produces an experience—which seems to them to be reality. As it turns out, it is a Distorted Reality.

This gets us back to where *you* might be right now.

Because of what has just happened to you—this huge change that has been visited upon you that is not something you would have chosen, that is something that just came down out of the blue, out of thin air—you're angry, or sad, or frustrated, or disappointed, or disillusioned, or "all of the above" . . . all because you are afraid. And you are afraid . . . all because you are in love. You're in love with yourself (even though you don't think you are) and you're in love with life (even though you say you hate it right now).

You're afraid of trading in a past that you knew for a future you do not. Afraid of what might happen. Afraid of how things could be. And afraid that you may never find this kind of situation again (this kind of job, this kind of person, this kind of home); that you may never have this kind of experience again.

Well, you *may* never find this kind of situation again—but you may very well have this kind of *experience* again. (For instance, you may never be with the same mate again, but you may very well have the same experience—the experience of joy and happiness—with another mate. It all depends on what you buy into: your Imagined Truth or the Apparent Truth.)

Remember that the experience of happiness has nothing to do with a given situation. This is hard to accept because we are absolutely certain that it does. Yet there is no connection between exterior events and interior experiences, except in your head.

Your capacity to know joy is not connected to this one person or to that one place of employment, for instance. You just *think* that it is. The Apparent Truth and the Imagined Truth are not identical. Ever.

Ever.

Events do not have meanings. Events are events, and meanings are thoughts. *Nothing* has any meaning *save the meaning you give it.* And the meaning you give to things does not derive from any event, circumstance, condition, or situation exterior to yourself. The Giving of Meaning is entirely an internal process.

Entirely.

Know Your Self as Light.
Bigger even, than Breath.
Larger even, than the Whole.
Quieter even, than the Quiet that holds You.

Know Your Self as Held.
Softer even, than as before;
Deeper even, than any Darkness.

When the Lightbody of You
breathes without borders
knows not
even of the concept
or of any bounds at all

When you Know Your Self
as only Light
summoning the Mystery
to move through You

exquisite, innocent instrument
of the long
long eternity of song

then

Know Your Self as
Life's greatest Laughter;
Life's greatest Lover,
beckoning the Mystery

come hither. . .

—*'Know Your Self as Light'* © 2006 Em Claire

10.

ALL ABOUT THE AFTEREFFECT

WHAT WE'VE BEEN TALKING about here is the technology of thought—or what I call the Mechanics of the Mind. And this exploration is more than you and I ambling down Philosophy Lane. When you deeply understand how your mind works, you will understand how to make it work for *you.*

This is something your mind does not want to do. Or, more accurately, it is something that your *ego* does not want you to do. Your ego is the part of your mind that thinks that *you are your mind.* And it knows that once you figure out how the mind works, you will become very clear that you are *not* your mind—and that with *that* knowledge will come the gradual disassembling of the ego in its present form.

Because the ego knows this, it will work overtime to get you to *take your mind off all this.* Somewhere in the next few chapters, for instance, it will try to cause you to feel "bored" with this entire exploration. Or "annoyed" that it's taking so long to be explained. Or "frustrated" that even after wading through the explanation, you're still not through with gathering what you need to know to change everything about the way to change the way you are experiencing change.

So watch your ego work here. Just watch your ego work on you to put this book down, to *just drop this whole line of inquiry.* If it succeeds, this wouldn't be the first time that your own ego has been your greatest enemy.

It is as that wonderful comic strip character, Pogo, created by the late Walt Kelly, used to say: "We have met the enemy, and they is us."

Now let me explain what the ego is and what it is not. The ego is the part of your mind that differentiates "you" from "everything else." As such, it is a vital part of the technology of thought. It is that part that can conceive not only of a thought, but of the thinker of the thought.

The ego is, therefore, one of your greatest gifts, because it allows you to experience "you" as *you*, and not everybody and everything else. The Actual Truth is that you ARE everybody and everything else . . . but the Part Of The All that calls itself "you" must be able to experience Itself *separately*, or It cannot do what It became physical to do; It cannot experience what it came to experience. Therefore, It *individuates* Itself—and the *ego* is the tool with which It does this.

The ego knows that Who You Really Are is bigger than the part of your self-awareness that resides only in your mind. In this, the ego is a great gift, a wonderful device, an incredible tool. Yet your ego can run amok, and when it does this it is like one of those runaway computers in science-fiction stories that suddenly thinks IT is *your master*, rather than you being its owner.

When your ego runs amok it not only continues to do the job of separating you from Everything Else, it separates you from *your Self.* It makes you think that you are IT, not that IT is a part of you. Your ego has then confused its job, imagining that it must protect you from knowing your very Self.

So when your ego tries to get you to feel bored, or that this narrative is not moving fast enough, that is your signal to get out of your mind. You need to be out of your mind to understand the Mechanics of the Mind and the System of the Soul. So just step away from your thoughts at that moment and keep reading. You will hear the incessant pleading of your ego to drop all this already, but *pay it no mind.*

Now I have said here that experience is not an outward thing, experience is an inward thing. That's why different people can have a different experience of the same event. Everybody's experience is the same only when people don't have time to think.

Whoops, wait a minute . . . *that* was an interesting idea. What was that—?

I *said* . . . when people don't have time to think, they become identical. They are driven to *react* rather than *respond*— as when people panic. Mass panic is virtually impossible to produce when people remain calm, stop, and think.

While I was writing this book a US Airways plane leaving New York City had birds fly into its engines, quickly and totally disabling it. That jetliner, piloted by a genuine hero, Captain Chesley B. "Sulley" Sullenberger, was forced to ditch in the Hudson River. After a picture-perfect emergency water landing, all 155 passengers on board left the plane and stood on its wings, waiting to be picked up by nearby boats. All survived. It was called a miracle. But the survivors said it like it is.

It was simple, they reported. Nobody panicked. Everybody kept a cool head. People were responding, rather than reacting.

In an article in *Newsweek* magazine a few weeks after the incident, Captain Sullenberger offered this personal observation: "We never gave up. Having a plan enabled us to keep our hope alive. Perhaps in a similar fashion, people who are in their own personal crises—a pink slip, a foreclosure—can be reminded that no matter how dire the circumstance, or how little time you have to deal with it, further action is always possible. There's always a way out of even the tightest spot. You can survive."

Thank you, Captain. You captured the essence of this whole book in a single paragraph. Wow. So the answer here, in *any* unwelcome and difficult situation where things are changing rapidly, is to stop and think. That whole process does not take long, by the way. Seconds, at most. Your mind is an amazing instrument. It can weigh all the options that are before you in nanoseconds and come up with a response. Yet it does take time. *Response* takes time, *reaction* is instantaneous.

Of course, it will do you little good to "stop and think" if your thoughts are based in Imagined Truth. Then your responses will be not much more elevated than raw reactions. If the passengers on that plane imagined that this was "it," this was the end, they were going to die, even if the plane landed safely on the water, they were soon going under, etc., etc., etc., panic would have ensued. Not enough can be said about the captain and the crew of that airliner, who kept people calm, cool, and collected.

So the trick is to raise your consciousness from the lowest to the highest level of awareness, *no matter what is going on around you.* Remember, *reactions* are instinctive, *responses* are thought out. That is, thoughts pushed outward.

Yet your thoughts have no shape or form or substance. They are as wisps of smoke. Not even that. They are *less* than smoke. They are simply *ideas* you hold. So, how to deal with that . . . ?

The funny thing about ideas is that they don't even have to be true to seem real. When it comes to a thought, your mind does not know the difference between what is real and what is imagined, between what is happening "now" and what was happening "then," between what is factually "true" and what is obviously "false."

So it is that you can watch a scary movie and your mind accepts the data as real, instructing your body to respond accordingly. Your heart starts racing, your breath becomes short, you may even perspire. Likewise, you can see a sensual photograph and experience bodily responses—even while knowing that the observed image is *just a picture.* It's what your mind *does* with the data, not the data itself, that produces your reaction. The event and your reality about it are not the same.

Your mind really *is* a mechanism. It is like a computer. Your laptop doesn't "care" about things, it merely responds to input—and to what has been put into it previously. There is a famous acronym used by computer techs: GIGO. It means, "Garbage In, Garbage Out."

Your mind operates in exactly the same way. It responds automatically to what you put into it—and if what you put into it is faulty data (that is, not based in Observed Reality or Ultimate Reality), your mind will come to faulty conclusions.

Now, if you base your *response* on such conclusions, you could be preparing yourself for a journey to emotional hell.

(Which is where you might be right now.) You could find yourself embroiled in thoughts having *nothing to do* with what is true. And it won't even matter to you—because you will not *know* that your thoughts are not true.

Until you do.

That's what this conversation is all about. What we are up to here is repeating, repeating, repeating the same thing; inputting, inputting, inputting the same data. Your mind *does* respond automatically to what you put into it—so what this book is about is putting into your mind *what you want it to respond to automatically.*

I just said, if what you put into your mind is faulty data (that is, not based in Observed Reality or Ultimate Reality), your mind will come to faulty conclusions. The reverse is also true. If what you put into your mind is *accurate* data (that is, based in Observed Reality or Ultimate Reality), your mind will come to accurate conclusions. *This will eliminate all manner of grief and anguish, turmoil and suffering, anger and fear from your life.*

So keep up with me now. As my mother used to say, "There's a method to my madness." This is all going to start coming together very quickly and you're going to see the elegance of the design, the perfection of how this all fits into one pattern, as you deal with the changes you are having to face now.

(If you have some questions, or there's something you'd like explained a little more fully, I invite you to go at any time to www.ChangingChange.net and see if you can find out what you need to know. Remember, this is a joint exploration. This is not like most books . . . read it and "get it" or not. This is a new kind of literature. This is *living* literature. So for heaven's sake, don't plow ahead here if your head is spinning and you need some help right now.)

Your thoughts create your emotions. We've now firmly established that. This means that *you* are creating your emotions. This is another very important piece of information. I can't say it enough.

Most people don't think they *create* their emotions. They think they just *have* them. Like snowflakes or raindrops, they fall out of the sky. People often say that they were just *overcome* by emotion.

In fact, emotions are chosen. The mind *decides* to feel a certain way. Emotions are an Act of Will.

Wow, that's tough. That's a tough one. That's very difficult for people to accept. You accept this and suddenly you're responsible for everything; for how you feel, for how you act with others as a result of how you feel . . . so when people hear this, they look for an "out."

("There must be *some* way in which I am not responsible for how I'm feeling. I mean, I can see that I'm responsible for what I *do* with my feelings, but my feelings themselves? *C'mon!* I can't be responsible for *that*. I feel the way I *feel*, dammit, and that's *just my truth*.")

Have you ever told yourself some version of that? Yet the human race can never evolve until we see the role we all play in the creation of our emotions. So I will repeat: emotions are chosen. The mind *decides* to feel a certain way. Emotions are an Act of Will.

Now I will concede this much: your mind does what it does *so fast* that it can *seem* as though you have no control over your emotions.

Your brain works faster than the fastest computer ever manufactured. (That may not be true in a few more years, but it is still true today . . . I think.) Your mind moves you very quickly into an emotion based on the thought it has formed. This is what is meant when people say, "I was very moved." Indeed they were. Thought is *energy*, and your mind's job is to *move that energy into motion* (E+motion).

Since this happens so doggone fast, so *lightning* fast, it becomes crucial that we know, *ahead of time*, the answer to what has now become the central question: What generates the thought that creates the emotion? Where does the thought *come from?*

If you can figure *that* out you will have gone a long way toward being able to *change* your thought about something. And if you can change your thought about something, you can create a different emotion around it—which will produce a different experience of it. As fast as the mind works, it still works only on the data it is working *with*. Garbage in/garbage out.

Bingo.

Bingo!

Because producing an experience different from the one you are now having is precisely what you want to do. I *promised* you that this was all going to get back around to *you*, to what is happening with *you*, right here, right now.

So . . . what creates a thought that creates an emotion? Where does a thought come from? It comes from your *inner truth*. And where does your inner truth come from? It comes from your *prior data*. So, knowing this ahead of time, can we change a thought that is likely to produce an unwelcome emotion before it produces that emotion?

Probably not. Maybe, in some rare instance, but in most cases, probably not. Because it happens too fast. It all happens so darned *fast*. Even knowing ahead of time *why* it's happening cannot stop it from happening *before you know it*. (I meant that literally!) Not unless you're a true Master. Not unless you're His Holiness, the Dalai Lama or somebody.

(And I'm not making fun of him. He really *is* a Master. But how many are there like him?)

So what's the point of all this . . . what's the use of us discussing this, exploring all this, examining this every which way from Sunday . . . ? Fair question. A really, really, *really* fair question. Such a fair, and important, question that it feels like this might be a good time, before plowing right ahead, to give yourself some

Breathing Space

Breathe into what you've just read, then . . . decide now if you want to go on, or rest with it for a while and meet with me here later. . . .

If you're ready to go on, drop down to . . .

IT'S AFTER, NOT BEFORE

The point of everything I've been telling you here is that, while you may not be able to use it to control your thoughts *ahead* of time, you now have an extraordinary tool, a powerful, *powerful* device, with which to change your thoughts *after the fact.* Indeed, almost *instantly* after the fact. And that is nearly as good as doing it ahead of time.

Think about it. If you could have changed most of the thoughts that created the negative emotions that you have had in the past twenty years within minutes, or even seconds, of having them, transforming them *on the spot* into something much more positive and healing, *wouldn't you have loved to have been able to do that?* I mean, do you think that would have changed some important moments in your life, *or what . . . ???*

Now think about this for your future—or even for the present moment in which you are now living. If you could transform negative emotions into positive emotions right now, and every day for the rest of your life—even if you did it *after you first felt* the negative emotion—wouldn't that be a wonderful gift?

I promised you at the outset—and I meant it when I promised—that when you're through here you'll be able to change Fear into Excitement, Worry into Wonder, Expectation into Anticipation, Resistance into Acceptance, Disappointment into Detachment, Enragement into Engagement, Addiction into Preference, Requirement into Contentment, Judgment into Observation, Sadness into Happiness, Thought into Presence, Reaction into Response, and a Time of Turmoil into a Time of Peace.

I didn't say you would never *have* fear, never *have* worry, never *have* disappointment or sadness or turmoil. I said that you would be able to *change them.* And you *will* be able to. You'll be able to change them fast. As fast as they arise. You can watch them come up, and you can change them as fast as they appear.

Or you can take your time with it. You can, as spiritual teacher Mary O'Malley suggests, just look at them with simple curiosity, and observe how it feels to have that particular feeling. Then you can hang out with your emotion—and the Distorted Reality that it generates—for as long as you want. You are in total control. You can create whatever "aftereffect" you wish. After you feel the first rush of emotion, how you wish it to affect you *is up to you.*

By the way, you can trust yourself on this. *You will know* when you're "done" having an experience. *You will know* when your period of mourning is over, your time of anger has passed, your veil of tears is ready to be lifted, your fear seeks to subside, your unhappiness feels complete.

Again, you can decide that this will be just moments after the very first impulse of negative energy flows through you—or you can choose to take weeks, months, or years. (We all know people who have been bitter for decades over an event in their past.) But now, at least, you cannot say that *you have no control* over these emotions or the thoughts that create them, that *you have no control* over the way you are experiencing your life, that *you have no control* over the reality in which you find yourself.

In my own life, I have reduced my experience of anger or frustration to about twelve to fifteen minutes. I just toss it away after that. Sadness takes a little longer. Sometimes a half-hour or more. Fear, longer still. I can hang out in fear, or waft in and out of it, for periods of time over days on end if I am not careful. And *melancholy?* Gosh, I could entertain melancholy as a Constant State of Mind given the slightest encouragement. (It's apparently too much fun for me to give up.)

The point: I hold on to the experiences that serve me, and only as long as they serve me. And how I can tell when they are no longer are serving me? By my Happiness Meter.

You see, I know myself pretty well. I can actually be *happy* being angry—and I am willing to admit that. I can be *happy* being sad, and I can admit that. There are certain times when it feels *good* to feel bad. There's a certain excitement attached to a particular kind of anger. (Self-righteousness is one of my favorites.) But when it no longer feels good to feel bad, I cut it off. *I will not disserve myself.*

You do not have to disserve yourself, either. So look at what is going on in your life right now, and see how you're feeling about it. As long as you feel good about feeling whatever you're feeling—as long as you are, at some level, getting a payoff out of it, enjoying the experience you are having—it is serving you. (The question is whether you will be able to admit that, even to yourself.)

As soon as you become clear that you are done feeling a certain way . . . when you hear yourself saying to yourself, *I'm finished with this. I'm through with this. I don't want any more of this!*, then you can use the tools that are being described on these pages to be *done with it*. Instantly.

That's the gift you're giving yourself here.

Let's make no mistake about something. You brought yourself to this book. You opened it. And it's you who've stayed with it through all of these deep explorations. *You've* done this. *You* have given yourself this gift. Nice going. Nice, nice going. You've needed it. You deserve it. And you got it.

Now I am going to show you exactly how all of this works in real life. Not on paper. Not in a lecture. In real life.

They don't set out to do anything grand.

They play, the three of them:
Black and Burr-ridden,
Speckled and Bright-eyed,
Sleek and Questioning.

Every morning the play continues,
tugging one another this way and that
along throughout a day.

If He sits, scratching and gazing out across
the great divide of valleys,
She will bring Him an enduring piece of hat
or garden hose or
the last fourth of a plastic ball
and drop it at His feet.

If the One with the moon-colored eyes
lies in the ivy, with sun on Her ribs
and leaves in Her ears
the other two will attack mid-dream
with nip and tug at
neck and tail.

It is pure genius and heart.

Three dogs living out the Mystery
every moment

while it slips like water

through all of my grasping.

—'Three Dogs Knowing' © 2005 Em Claire

11.

NOTICE THE MOMENT

I'M GOING TO DEMONSTRATE to you how you can—
how any person can—move to a new inner truth about anything, how you can upshift from Imagined Truth to Apparent
Truth in minutes.

You can use this technique either *before* a moment occurs
(as in the case of stepping into something that you know is
likely to happen) or *after* a moment occurs (as will be the case
most often, I should think).

Elevating your inner truth is a matter of changing your
perspective, and this is easier than most people realize. In fact,
it can be done very quickly.

As my demonstration here I'm going to use an example
from one of the Changing Everything workshops that I present
around the world. In this workshop I use a process with people that I call *Notice the Moment*. (It is just one of several

processes that I have created to invite the mind to a new level of awareness.)

The *Notice the Moment* tool awakens the mind and allows it to restart the thought process by inviting the mind to notice that *Then* is not *Now* and that *Now* is not *Tomorrow*, but that *Now* is NOW. In other words, the mind is invited to pay attention to what is readily apparent, rather than to what is clearly imagined.

This process shows the mind that there's *nothing going on* except *what's going on.* It instructs the mind to stop adding things to that. The data that is then considered is limited to the data that is observed, that is readily apparent. This creates a new starting point for thought: the Apparent Truth.

From this new thought arises a new emotion. The new emotion produces a new experience, the Observed Reality, to replace the Distorted Reality that is causing so much inner turmoil. All of this transformation is occurring in a person's interior. The exterior event has not changed.

I use the *Notice the Moment* process when I find that someone in my workshop is continually using a false starting point for their thought about what is happening in the moment, thus creating a distorted experience of Now.

Classic examples of this are the people in a retreat or workshop who become angry because something has changed in the room. They came into the workshop feeling all excited and happy to be there. They're filled with the anticipation of having a powerful experience. Then something happens. Something changes. Maybe I've said something that somebody doesn't like. Or maybe I've exhibited a characteristic that rubs someone the wrong way. The mood of the room changes. You can feel it in the air. You can *feel* this change. It's palpable and it's real.

All it takes is one participant to have negative feelings for the energy of the room to change. Sooner or later that participant will say, "I don't like what's going on here." I will then ask, "What do you think is happening?"

My question often sounds strange to them. I explain that many people have a difficult time *noticing the moment*—and so when I ask them what is happening right now, they don't know how to answer.

So I say to that person, "You said there is something you don't like. What do you think is going on right now?"

They might say, "Well, you're starting to get real sharp in your tone of voice and very controlling," or something like that.

So I say, "Is that how you perceive what I'm doing? And even if it is what I am doing, so what?"

"So, I'm not *happy*," they'll repeat again.

Right about then I'll invite them to the front of the room by asking, "Would you like to heal that?" Often they'll respond with something like, "Heal what? I'm totally fine. It's you who's acting like an ass."

The room chuckles and I chuckle (because it happens in every retreat that someone in the room turns on the facilitator) and then I say, "Well, maybe you can heal *me*. Would you be willing to do that? Would you be willing to help me be less of an ass?"

Now even they are smiling. "I guess so," they may allow.

So I say, "Fabulous! Thank you! So let's try something. Come on up here with me."

And they do. Warily, I might add. But they do. Because one thing about most people that I've met is that they are willing to "play." Most people are pretty courageous. Most people are very brave. In fact, you're like that. You know how I know that you're like that? *Because you're reading this book right now.* Only a brave person would do that. I'm talking about a person who is emotionally brave. That's you, or you wouldn't be looking at the stuff we're talking about here. So thanks for being here with me.

That's just what I say to the person who has come to the front of the room, too. I say, "Thanks for being here with me." Then I say, "I'm going to ask you now to *notice the moment.*"

They usually respond, "I don't know what that means. What do you mean?"

"I mean, look closely at what's happening right now, here in the room, while you're standing here with me. This is a very safe process. Can I do this with you? Do I have permission to do this process with you?"

I tell them that it may at some level be revealing or maybe even a tiny bit startling, but it will not be damaging in any way. If they say yes, okay, you can run the process, here's how it often goes . . . this is from an actual workshop transcript of my interaction with a lady who had become a bit put off—*annoyed* might be a better word—by my energy:

Me: Are you sure you are willing to proceed with the process?
Retreat Participant: Yes, I am.
Me: Absolutely sure?
Participant: Yes, I'm absolutely sure.

Me: And you won't get mad at me, no matter what happens, so long as I don't hurt you—?

Participant: No, I won't get mad at you. No more mad than I now am. (The room laughs.)

Me: Great. So as I talk to you about this process I want you to understand that nothing is going to happen that . . . AAAAARG!! RAAAAAHHHH!

I *yelled* right in her face.

I yelled very loud, a foot and a half from her. Less, actually. I got right in her face and *screamed* something . . . just a sudden sound, an utterance.

Of course, she jumped back. She was just blown away, and tears came to her eyes.

I gently said, "What happened just now?"

She looked at me as if I were from Mars. She was still weeping a little, and softly shaking. Again I said, very softly, "Notice the moment. What just happened here?"

"You scared me."

"No, no, no, *you* scared you. What did *I* do? *You* scared you, what did *I* do?"

"You yelled at me. You moved closer to me and screamed in my face."

"Okay, what does that look like to you? What exactly occurred? What do you *observe* to have happened as opposed to what your mind is *telling you about* what happened? What is apparent here, as opposed to what you imagined?"

"I didn't imagine anything! You stepped right up to me and yelled in my face! You scared the hell out of me."

"No, I did not scare you. You scared you. Danger was the Distorted Reality. But what was the Observed Reality?"

"I don't understand what you're driving at. I don't know what you want me to say."

"What did you *see?* What did you observe?"

"A loud voice, a loud sound hit my ear."

"Good. What else?"

"I felt your breath. You were so close, I felt your breath in my face."

"Good. Now we're getting there. Did I touch you?"

"No."

"Did I hurt you in any physical way?"

"No."

"So what happened is that a loud noise reached your ear and you felt breath in your face. Is that what happened?"

"Yes."

"So what? Why would that be scary? If it startled you for a moment, that's fair. You hear a clap of thunder and it startles you, but after the initial start, what about that would cause you any level of trauma?"

"You don't *get it.* You scared the hell out of me."

"But you started crying. You broke into tears."

"Yes! *Because you scared the hell out of me!*"

"No, *you* scared you. But let's not argue the point. Let me ask you this. Have you ever been startled by thunder—like a bolt of thunder in the night?"

"Yes, of course. I'm sure we all have."

"Good. And when that happened, did you burst into tears?"

Silence.

Then . . .

"No."

"Okay. So we can establish that being startled for the moment, because something fell or you heard a clap of thunder or something happened, is normal if you weren't expecting it. But only a baby actually cries when he hears the thunder— *because he doesn't know what is happening.* You don't cry when you hear thunder, even if it startles you momentarily. Why? Because you know what is happening. Your mind goes to the *apparency of things.* Not to the Imagined Truth, but to the Apparent Truth. After the moment of non-expectation has passed, what would cause you any level of continuing trauma?"

Right about here I began to see the faint light of recognition crossing the retreat participant's face. I went on. . . .

"The continuing trauma that you experience in any moment of Now is stuff that you start pouring into that moment, instantly, from somewhere else, not from The Here And Now. You reach for something that is not real, such as, for instance, 'yesterday.' Your mind knows: My dad did that to me when I was six. You start pouring yesterday into this moment. Pull the plug out from that tank of data and let them all drain out. Drain the Moment of Now of yesterday. Can you do that?"

A pause. Then . . .

"Yes, I think I can—how did you know about my father?"

"It was a guess. It could have been anything. The point is, your mind pulled something forward out of the past and into This Moment, and it's that thought that created the emotion that produced your experience of being scared as hell. Now, look again at the moment that just passed, right here in this room. What happened? What did you observe?"

"I observed a loud sound, a loud voice, so loud that it startled me. I observed breath on my face. I felt threatened."

"Good. That's a good looking. You're working well. Now tell me, are you afraid of me? Do you think that I, as the facilitator of this retreat, am likely to hurt you in any way?"

"No. Probably not."

"*Probably* not?"

"Definitely not. You're not going to hurt me."

"Are you certain about that?"

"Yes."

"Then why would you feel threatened in any way?"

"Because you remind me of my father, who *did* hurt me when he yelled like that."

Here there is a long pause. She noticed this before, but now she really gets it. The whole *room* gets it.

Finally I said, as softly as I could. . . .

"I see. So you think that *Now* is *Then*."

"I'm sorry. It was an automatic reaction."

"Don't be sorry, it's very normal. But let me ask you this: Do you think you can 'un-automatic' it?"

"Yes, I probably can."

"You mean I could yell in your face again and you wouldn't feel threatened?"

"I think so. Yes, that's right."

"Could someone else?"

"What?"

"Could someone else, at some other time, yell at you suddenly and you not feel threatened?"

"I suppose so, yes."

"Why? Why do you suppose you would be able to do that in the future when you were not able to do that just now?"

"Because I've just had it shown to me, through this process, what I'm doing. Because I see now that what I *think* is happening is not what is happening."

"Great. So you're managing to discern the difference between Then and Now. You're freeing yourself of yesterday. You don't owe it any more of your todays. You've given it enough of your now moments. So all you have to do to bring yourself this freedom always is . . . *notice the moment.* Look closely at exactly what is going on. Right here, right now. Don't buy into the Imagined Truth, move into the Apparent Truth. Got it?"

"Yes, I think I do."

"You *think* you do?"

"No, I do. I've got it."

"Great. Thank you very much. And later in this retreat, if I start to get excited and raise my voice or use a sharp tone, you'll understand what is happening and what is not, right?"

(Laughter.) "Right."

"Terrific. Please sit down."

(Applause.)

Believe me, you don't have to know.

Not so much that you render yourself helpless.
Helpless in the face of what Life brings next.

So make peace with knowing very little.

About Love.

About Others.

About how life *should* be.

Make amends with how things are.

Not knowing a thing,
walk with gentle knees,
ready to drop to them, at any moment
that Life dictates it.

Keep an empty hand
so that it can be brought to your heart
when a grief arrives.

Make up a bed that you can fall into
as your own, comforting arms.

———

We come to find that Life is mostly quiet.
It asks us to *live by our Knowing*, while
surrendering that very same thing.

It vibrates easily around us,
candid and benevolent.

You see, it's only
when we root ourselves solid in some knowing again,
that Life seems to have to shout—

rises,

lovingly,
from Its whisper.

—'*Life Is Mostly Quiet*' © 2007 Em Claire

12.

WHERE OUR TRUTH COMES FROM

I HOPE THAT YOU noticed that all I was doing in the process I just shared with you was simply encouraging that lady to start her thinking at a new Point of Origin. She was invited to place her Apparent Truth, rather than her Imagined Truth, at the beginning of her thought process.

When I screamed in her face she actually had Three Brands of Truth to select from as she formed her thought about what was going on. By choosing one of those truths she formed a thought which created an emotion which produced her reality. First she produced a Distorted Reality. Eventually she elevated her experience to the Observed Reality. She did it all by simply *changing her mind*.

Do you see what else "workshop lady" was doing just then? She was doing what we are *all* doing all the time. She was creating her own reality. Reality is not what's happening, it's what we *think* is happening. We don't experience what's going on outside, we experience what's going on *inside* about what's going on outside.

Many people think that "you create your own reality" is a spiritual doctrine. Yet this business of creating one's own reality is not something that is done at what most people think of as a spiritual level. It is done at a psychological level. It is a function of the mind. It has to do with the Mechanics of the Mind.

Now that you understand exactly how this happens, you will be able to *make* it happen. At will. And then . . . you'll be free. Free of emotional turmoil, free of anguish and frustration and anxiety and fear—the unwelcome emotions that so often accompany unwanted change and life disruptions.

When I was a kid in the fifth grade there was this bully who would not leave me alone. Every day he'd find a reason to bump me in line or on the stairs or in the lunchroom or wherever. And every day I'd say something like, "Stop it! You'd better *stop it.*" And I can remember to this day him sneering at me and saying, "Yeah? Whaddya gonna make of it, huh . . . *huh?*"

Of course, he was being very wise. Without knowing it, but very wise nonetheless. Because he was asking the quintessential question of all of life, and about every change that occurs within it. *What are you going to make of it?*

This is life's inquiry every time something happens on the outside of our mind. Every time any event occurs. Every time something goes down. Whatever it is. It doesn't matter. It could be that a relative dies. It could be that you've lost your glasses. It could be that your spouse is in a bad mood. Or in a very *good* mood. It could be that you've just been laid off. Or just been hired. Always, always, the question from Life is the same:

What are you going to make of it?

Your answer creates your experience.

Most of us don't see it that way, but that's exactly what's going on every moment of our lives. We are receiving incoming data from the outside world and we are creating our reality out of it.

We are creating that reality quite literally out of thin air. We are creating it out of pure thought, and that thought emerges from the *truth* that we hold in our mind. All of which leads us to the next logical inquiry. *Where does that truth come from?*

First we asked, where does reality come from? And the answer was: it emerges out of our experience. Then we asked, where does our experience come from? And the answer was: it emerges out of our emotion. Then we asked, where does our emotion come from? And the answer was: it emerges out of our thought. Then we asked, where does our thought come from? And the answer was: it emerges out of our truth. Now we ask, where does our truth come from? And the answer is: it emerges *out of our data.*

And where does our data come from? Well, it is generously supplied to us by many sources. Our parents. Our family. Our friends. Our neighbors. Our teachers. Our models. Our culture. Our religion. Our entertainments. Our games. And all of our own previous actual "on-the-ground" encounters with life—all of which have, in turn, been affected by *all of the above.*

Then we ask . . . what stimulates, what causes, the "bringing forward" of all this past data to our awareness? And the answer is: an Event. A happening. An occurrence outside of your mind. All events call up Past Data.

And THEN we ask: What causes *The Event?* And the answer is: Our Reality.

In other words, *one thing leads to another.* In still other words, *the whole thing is a circle.*

Are you *getting* this? That straight line . . . the Line of Causality? . . . that line is not straight at all. It is a *circle.*

There are no straight lines in the universe. They only look straight. All lines ultimately curve in on themselves. Ever look "as far as the eye can see"? You're looking into thin air! The earth is *curved.* Beyond the horizon, it *curves.* Everything is curved. Time. Space. Everything, not just the horizon. What I am referring to now is what is called the *Event Horizon.*

Okay, here again is our Line of Causality . . .

event + data + truth + thought + emotion = experience = reality

Now, in your mind's eye, *bend this line around* so that the two ends meet in the back, like a watch band. Then you will see the truth. Events touch Realities which touch Events which touch Realities which touch Events which touch Realities which . . .

They butt up against each other.

Oh, boy . . . this is doing more than bending the Line of Causality. This is *mind bending.*

Whew.

Okay . . . I need a little break here. I really do. I mean, I'm *writing* this and I need a little break. How must it be on *your* end . . . ? So . . .

Let's take a short break.

Breathe into what you've just read, maybe review it a time or two . . . then, put it on the back burner and let it simmer.

Only if you're ready to go on, drop down to . . .

WHAT DO WE HAVE TO GO ON?

Are you able to see yet how any of this could apply to you? Are you starting to put together how your experience of what is happening right now in your life could be changed dramatically by understanding—and then using—the mechanism I've been describing here?

All you have to do is change your innermost truth about what is happening. Begin your thinking in a new place. Yet here is a new challenge. . . .

There is no clean starting point. No fresh perspective.

Someone once said, "Within human life no fresh perspective is possible after Day One." That may be a bit of an exaggeration, but the point is clear. We are almost always coming from Prior Data when considering any given moment. How else could it be? We have nothing to *go on* except what's been *going on.*

Or *do* we . . . ?

What creates your thought is the "truth" you buy into. And what determines the truth you buy into—Apparent Truth or Imagined Truth—is *which past data you look at.*

Here we go, deeper and deeper down the rabbit hole. Soon the Mad Hatter will appear, swearing to us that what is so is not so, and that what is not so is so. Here we go, deeper and deeper into the Matrix. Soon the Man in the White Suit will take us to the White Room with all the television screens and explain it all to us. . . .

What we will learn is not only that it is from your Past Data that your innermost truth emerges, but from *the choice you make* of the Past Data you select to look at.

During the truth-creation process (yes, your mind *creates* the truth, it does not observe it) the mind travels backward in time to retrieve every piece of data from all previous moments that look, feel, taste, sound, or smell like this moment. If the mind finds a match, it compares the two data to see just how close the match is, then *adds to the present moment* all information from the past *that it considers relevant*, thereby creating *a whole new set of data not at all resembling the data that was originally observed.*

This revised and supplemented data is enormously influential in producing what you call your "experience." Your "reality" is not what you are seeing, but what you *think* you are seeing after you have added past data. It is based on the "truth" that your mind has extracted from your Past Data and exported to the Present Moment. It is "reality" as *you* have experienced it. Ten other people may have experienced it in ten other ways. This is important to always keep in mind. To *always* keep in mind.

Now comes the tricky part. The fact is that you hold in your mind *two kinds* of Past Data. I'm going to call this *Judged Past Data* and *Factual Past Data.*

Wouldn't it be wonderful if things just came in ones? But no, we have to have the Triune Reality and the Three Brands of

Truth, and now we get down to the two kinds of Past Data. But at least this is the bottom of it. This is the real culprit.

If there were only one kind of Past Data we would have only one brand of Truth and only one version of Reality. So at least now we know what the problem is!

Now . . . Judged Past Data can contain what you call Good Memories or Bad Memories, the labels depending upon how you judged the events that originally produced those memories . . . which, of course, was a judgment based on *prior* events viewed within the context of *prior* Judged Past Data . . . which, in turn, was based on even more prior events . . . and so on, right back to your birth—and beyond. (Yes, you began taking in data about what was going on around you *in the womb*.)

An example of Judged Past Data: the breakup of a romantic relationship is painful.

An example of Factual Past Data: the breakup of a relationship is the end of the time that two people will spend together in intimate living arrangements. This can be either "bad" or "good" . . . or neither, but just what's so.

All of this stuff is rolling around in your mind all of the time. It resides there, and it cannot be deleted. There is no delete button on this computer. Your mind will "bring to front" this Past Data the moment any Present Data looks even a little like it. You will then make an assessment of the Present Data based on prior data that you, and only *you*, possess. Nobody else is walking around with your past. Nobody else has your history.

This means that no one else in the universe can encounter, understand, or experience anything at all in precisely the way you do. *Not so long as you stay in your mind.* In strictly literal terms, it is impossible to have a "meeting of minds." You can, however, have a blending of *souls*. This is the blessed relationship for which every human yearns. This is where the truth is known. Humans yearn for this blessed relationship because they have a cellular awareness that not only is it possible, not only has it happened, but it is happening *right now*. The only thing standing in the way of our *experiencing* this relationship is the Emotion that is based on the Thought that is based on the Truth that is based on Judged Past Data.

How is it possible for the soul to sidestep this Line of Causality when the mind apparently cannot? Simple. In Ultimate Reality (where the soul resides) *there is no such thing as Past Data*. It is always Right Here, Right Now.

Ah, but that is a whole different discussion, saved for part 2.

Returning to the human experience of what is happening in most people's lives, we see that our minds are constantly rolling around in Judged Past Data or Factual Past Data, producing, at the end of the Line of Causality, what psychiatrists and psychologists label Objective Reality and Subjective Reality.

Subjective Reality emerges from *Judged* Past Data. (Not all of this is negative, by the way, and that should not be inferred. Often we judge prior events as having been quite wonderful.) Objective Reality emerges from *Factual* Past Data. (What you might call "raw data" as opposed to "analyzed data.")

In my own model I call Objective Reality "Observed Reality," and I label Subjective Reality "Distorted Reality." Why don't I use the same terms that the therapeutic community uses? Why have I created my own model?

Because my terminology is more descriptive and, more important, because the traditional therapeutic model *does not recognize the existence of a third reality.*

Everything came together for me when I started looking at life using a model that showed something *above* Distorted Reality and Observed Reality—something that I labeled Ultimate Reality.

The existence of this third reality is what makes it possible for all people to dramatically change their lives. Not merely alter their lives, but *transform* them.

Paying attention to the second reality—what you objectively observe, as opposed to what you subjectively experience—can certainly alter one's experience for the better, and good psychologists have helped people do that. But paying attention to the third reality—what is *ultimately* happening as opposed to what we *observe* to be happening—can so affect your life that you may never have to endure emotional turmoil again. *Ever.*

This is where Buddha lived. This is where Christ resided. This is where all true Masters live. It was the home of Paramahansa Yogananda. It is the home of the Dalai Lama. It is where you will find Thich Nhat Hanh. And Western masters too, such as Stephen Levine, Eckhart Tolle, Byron Katie, and Mary O'Malley. These are people who *understand*, and who some say have *mastered life.*

I have put this understanding in my own words. To me it seems clear that to really utilize the mind at optimal levels (and, hence, experience *life itself* at those levels) we must move beyond the standard therapeutic model.

Modern psychological constructs hold very little space (if any) for spirituality. That is to say, for *God* and for the *soul. This is a supreme irony* since the original idea was exactly the opposite!

The very word "psychology" gives us our clue. "Psyche" comes from the Greek word meaning "soul." "Logy" is also Greek, and means "knowledge." We see that "psycho+logy"= "soul knowledge"—which is what the ancient Greeks knew that all healthy behavior was anchored in!

The constructs that I employ (including those in this book) know the same thing. The model I use to study and affect behaviors is *based* in spirituality; it has its *foundation* in theo+logy—that is, knowledge of God. Does this make it therapeutically more effective? *What do you think?*

In my observation the third reality, Ultimate Reality, emerging as it does from Actual Truth, finally offers an explanation (that neither of the first two realities does) for not only *what* is going on, *but why*. And once we know *why* something is happening (sudden change, for instance), we can employ the immense power of the mind, combined with the eternal clarity of the soul, to not only alter our experience of what *has happened*, but to create our experience of what *will happen*.

This is the next evolutionary step for humankind. And humans do not have to wait years to take it. You, yourself, can take this step in *minutes*. Indeed, in the time required to finish this book.

And here's the best thing. You don't have to share my point of view about God in order to do it. You don't have to believe in God at all. You're free. This book does not seek your religious conversion. I'm not going to try to convince you of anything here. I've simply been sharing some tools with you. You'll see if they work for you or not, but you don't have to believe in anything in order to use them.

But know that what will change here, should you use these tools, is not just your experience of the life change that you are moving through right now. These tools will also impact all the changes that you will experience from now until the day you die—when you will undergo the Biggest Change of All.

When you die, what will happen to you, what you will become aware of, will change everything about the way you view the life you have lived. Every event will be viewed from a larger perspective, every moment will be viewed with love and acceptance, every misstep will be viewed with understanding and compassion, every achievement will be viewed with sweet pride and soft joy and a willingness, at last, to accept and embrace one's own magnificence.

The conversation we are now having is about *bringing that same view forward*. It is about moving it from Then to Now.

I can remember my father saying, "If I knew *then* what I know *now*. . . ." This is about knowing "now" what you will know "then." Exciting, yes?

All of This:
it is preparation for walking in the world
as Light.
You have been found now,
and the running of many lifetimes
is over.

So as each layer of dust
is wiped clean
from the surface,
the You
you have known

must disperse.

Let *this* Light become
Your speech & Your silence.

Let the grief
that has lived you,
pass away.

Let the people
who love You,
love Themselves.

Let the earth shake,
the stars burn
the skies break
when You do.

As painful as this part is,

You were meant to know your Light.

—'*You Were Meant*' © 2007 Em Claire

13.

OF SNAKES AND
LIONS AND HUMANS, TOO

WE ARE VERY NEAR the end of part 1 of this book. This first half of this wonderful conversation brought us into deep focus on the Mechanics of the Mind in order that you might change the way you experience change. In the second half of our time together we will look at changing the way you *create* change, by exploring the System of the Soul.

It would have been impossible to explain how the second—and more exciting—tool works without us deeply understanding the mechanics of the first. And it will be impossible to fully utilize the first, no matter how thoroughly we explain it, without the fuel (that is to say, the *power*) that the second *gives* to the first.

All of which is to notice that life in *both* its parts has a purpose and a function just the way it is. We are truly served by using life in all the ways that it presents itself, physical and spiritual, as a means and a pathway to the Ultimate Reality.

So now we shall go just one more, final, layer deep in exploring life in the physical—for this final exploration will lead to *a life-altering question* that will make everything you have read in the past several chapters usable and workable in a way that you might never have imagined.

As we do this I will come right back to you and your experience of life on this day.

All along I have been presuming that on this day you are standing in what I call "the middle of a moment" of significant change in your life. I hope you now see that, fascinatingly, your *experience* of this change may have nothing to do with what you actually saw, felt, tasted, heard, or smelled. It's your Past Data that formed your innermost truth about it, and it is from your innermost truth that your thought, emotion, and experience emerges producing your present reality.

Is it a Distorted Reality, the Observed Reality, or is it the Ultimate Reality in which you stand? Well, you can tell by how you *feel*.

If you feel terrible, you are standing in a Distorted Reality. If you feel just fine, you are standing in the Observed Reality. If you feel blissful, you are standing in the Ultimate Reality.

All of this depends on what kind of match your mind is finding for the data that exists in this present moment. But now let's ask an intriguing question. What if you encounter in your life a piece of here-and-now data for which your mind *cannot find a match*?

I ask the question because, as a person who is thinking this all through with me, you may have already asked it in your own mind. The answer is that this situation is highly unlikely.

As I've noted before, it is virtually impossible to not find some kind of match in Past Data for what is going on now. Almost everything that you are experiencing is a version of something you have experienced before. Granted, it may have been as far back as the crib (and therefore perhaps out of your conscious memory), but it is there in your data bank, I assure you.

In my own case, to give you an example, I happen to vividly remember a time when I was under two years old and standing in my crib. I was just being potty trained and I needed to go to the bathroom. I called for my mom, who was in another room, to lift me out of the crib. She heard me and said, "I'll be right there, sweetheart." But she never came.

I called and called, and then began to cry. She kept calling back to me that she was coming, but she was taking a terribly long time. I don't know what she was doing in that other room, but it was something that she clearly did not want to be interrupted. The trouble was, that exact moment was when I needed her. I knew that she heard me because she called back to me. But she was not coming. I felt abandoned. *Why wasn't she coming?*

I tried and tried to get out of the crib . . . I can still see myself trying to hoist myself up, then working to lift my leg up over the railing . . . but it was no use, it was too high. I couldn't get out.

MAH-MEE I cried one last time, but it was no use. Finally, through a lake of tears, I had no choice but to soil my diaper.

Now look, I know that this was not a Big Deal. *Now* I know that. But *then* I did not know that. And *then* is when *the data was stored.*

You see? You understand?

I had been told that Big Boys use the potty. I was devastated at having failed to be a Big Boy.

To this day I have had to deal with abandonment issues. You think I am making this up? *This is how it works!* This is *how the mind works.* It does not know the difference between Then and Now.

I can't erase this memory. In fact, the harder I tried through the years, the more indelible the memory became. Of course. I was *burning it in there.* And it is as I said before. There is no delete button on this machine.

So . . . it is highly unlikely—not impossible, but very unlikely—that your mind will not be able to find a match in Past Data for a Present Moment encounter. Your mind will do its best to find *something* to match it up with because your mind understands that your survival *depends* on it finding something to compare Now with. Otherwise, how will you know how to proceed?

But let us say that it just cannot. Let us say that something that's occurring right now is so unique, so unusual, so first-of-its-kind, that you truly have nothing at all from any yester-moment with which to compare it.

Not to worry. Your mind will search a "sub-directory" in your memory comprised of data that is held beneath the first level of consciousness, in your molecular encoding—or your "subconscious." This is called your *cellular memory*—or what some people refer to as *instinct.* (This is where "fight-or-flight" comes from, among other reactions.)

Actually, your mind went to this sub-directory first. It does that as the first means of self-preservation, just in case you don't have time to think. In the moment that any outward event occurs, your initial impulse will be to react instinctively. Then, if you *do* have time to think (Remember when we talked about this before? We said this only takes seconds. Nanoseconds, really) you can decide how you wish to *respond*, rather than how you would *react* if you hadn't thought about it.

Response Time is a luxury. Reaction Time is instant. Yet when you respond, always know that you are never responding to what is happening now. You are responding to your past. Again, so that you are clear . . . if your Past Data really and truly can produce no match whatsoever to your Present Data, you will revert back to instinct—which is *also* Past Data. It is simply Past Data of a different sort.

Your *instinct* is what pushes you into your future. It says, if you want a future, listen to your past—even if it is a past that you cannot consciously remember. Your cellular memory, this "sub-directory," holds *the history of your entire species.* So if *anyone* in your biological line has encountered data about what you are now witnessing, *that data will immediately be made available to you.*

This is the Reptilian Brain at work.

The what?

Yes, I said the Reptilian Brain. And all of this—*all of it*—relates directly to the experience that you are having right now, on this very day. This short course in the Mechanics of the Mind is something that should be taught in every school, in age-appropriate ways, so that when we all become adults we know what we are dealing with here—and can create the lives we always imagined we would lead.

So . . . our last lesson in part 1 of this book, together with a dialogue to illustrate it, is next. If you'd like to take a little rest first, this would be a great time to

Put the book down and rest your mind for a bit

If you're ready to go on, drop down to . . .

THE FINAL LESSON:
YOUR MAGNIFICENT BRAIN

The tool of the mind is the brain. This magnificent instrument has developed in stages, through the process of evolution. First we had a Reptilian Brain. Then the evolution of the species produced a Mammalian Brain, stacked on top of that. Finally, we evolved the Human Brain.

(I want to acknowledge here that I owe much of what I am now sharing with you to the genius and insight of Dr. Ilchi Lee, a Korean master whose several books on the human brain are highly recommended.)

A reptile does not make value judgments. It does not take in data from the present moment, match it with data from similar moments, analyze the data to see how it compares, and make a decision on how to respond based on its assessment of relative values. A reptile responds to everything instinctively. Its information is *cellular*. It is *inherited*. Its response will therefore be identical from one encounter to the next, given similar exterior stimuli, changing only over centuries as evolution demands. This instinctive reaction is instantaneous, and all snakes of identical species react identically to identical stimuli.

The human mind works instantaneously, too, but it performs many more functions in the same infinitesimal amount of time, because our brains have evolved to a much higher level of functionality. Our brains also hold specific data that is exclusive to us. No one else *on earth* has a mind like yours. So it is that all humans, while also members of the same species, do not react identically to the same stimuli.

A snake does not experience anger. Did you know that? You can't make a snake "mad." You can't make a snake "happy," either. A snake is simply in an eternal state of being what it is. A snake. It has, in this sense, completed its evolutionary journey and is now experiencing Being in Fullness.

Humans are on the same Journey to Fullness, yet we have not completed our trek. We have not come to the end of our evolutionary process.

I should acknowledge that this is a subject of some controversy. There are those anthropologists who believe that we *have* completed our evolutionary journey. They argue that humans have evolved as far as they are going to.

In fact, this is the *prevailing* idea among the world's preeminent biologists. *Discover* magazine tells us so in a cover story in March 2009 by contributing editor Kathleen McAuliffe, winner of a 2009 Alicia Patterson Journalism Fellowship to continue her research into human evolution from the Stone Age to the present. "This view has become so entrenched that it is practically doctrine," McAuliffe reports.

Yet she also says that now there is some significant disagreement from some significant sources. She informs us that a team of researchers is now suggesting that "over the past

10,000 years, human evolution has occurred a hundred times more quickly than in any period in our species' history."

This lines up perfectly with my own observation that change is increasing exponentially on our planet. There are a lot of reasons for this, including the increase in the speed with which we communicate that I have mentioned here, and McAuliffe's deeply insightful article offers some additional fascinating hypotheses (*Are We Still Evolving?*, March 2009, *Discover*).

So it is my hypothesis that humans are still seeking to fully be who they are. I observe myself and I observe humanity and it feels as if we are not even halfway to that goal. Or to put it another way, *we don't know the half of it.* This idea can be depressing or exhilarating, depending on how you look at it. (The same is true, by the way, of all of life.)

I, for one, am exhilarated. As magnificent as we humans are, we have halfway more to go! The potential of tomorrow stretches as far as our vision can carry us . . . and way, way beyond. But . . . enough of my waxing philosophic. Let's get back to our explanation of the brain. . . .

A lion, as opposed to a snake, has a Mammalian Brain. It can, and does, experience anger. (Don't test this theory. I promise you, it's accurate.) But a lion does not make a judgment about these things. "Was my anger justified? Was it righteous or misplaced? Was it perfect or overblown? Should I get angry at that level in the future? What will the other lions think?" Lions don't ask themselves such questions.

A human has a brain developed to the third level. A human takes in data, compares it to other data, organizes ways of responding to that data, weighs all the options, analyzes the possible and probable outcomes attached to each option, makes a judgment about the best of those outcomes, and tells the body how to respond. All in one /one-millionth of a second.

Pretty incredible, eh? Yet even with all this magnificent computing equipment housed in your skull, the response your mind selects *may have nothing to do with the moment at hand.* Now isn't *that* cute. . . .

The problem is that many humans have not learned yet to use *all* the faculties of the mind—including the ability to consider information *not contained in any prior data*—to produce their response to any given situation. Much less have they considered using *the exact same mechanism*, the human brain, to *create* conditions that they prefer, rather than endure conditions they encounter.

All that most of our poor minds do is bring up memories and sub-memories from our recent (this lifetime) and distant (evolutionary lifeline) past. It dumps these data into our Now and simultaneously projects them onto our Future.

This lightning-quick process creates energy in a form that we call "thought" and sends it into motion. I formulate this phenomenon as: E+motion. For the purposes of this discussion I call it, simply, *emotion.*

This is the creative force of the universe.

I think I need to say that again.

This is the creative force of the universe. That it why it is so sad that so many people think that emotions are things over which they have no control. In fact, it is as I said earlier: emotions are chosen. The mind *decides* to feel a certain way. Emotions are an Act of Will. Only when we understand this can we do as I have described . . . use emotion to create conditions we prefer, rather than simply react to conditions we endure. (More on this—*much* more—in part 2 of this discussion.)

We've already explored at length how to change your emotion. A simple recap: change the thought that sponsors it. To do *that*, change the truth that sponsors the thought. To do *that*, use your mind to its fullest potential in the moments immediately after any given event. *Search beyond your Data Bank to create a basis for your truth.* (Again, that is what part 2 of this book is all about.)

I have gone deeply into the Mechanics of the Mind here in order to give you a real basis for understanding how to use them to go beyond them.

Can you see now more clearly that this is all that the lady in the workshop did? She did it rather quickly, too, with just the tiniest facilitation. Furthermore, she agreed that she could probably do this in the future on her own, without prompting or help of any kind—because she suddenly saw what she had been doing. She consciously watched herself pouring what she judged to be a bad past into the present, projecting a memory of her father all over it.

In seeing this, she was doing what spiritual teacher Mary O'Malley and others call "bearing witness." Workshop Lady witnessed what she was creating in her mind and simply made a new choice about that. Now she doesn't have to do that anymore.

The process I've been describing is about moving to a new thought. And so it's perfect that the work that I and others like Eckhart Tolle and Mary O'Malley do in the world is sometimes described as being part of the New Thought Movement. It is about *raising consciousness,* or *elevating awareness,* from

Imagined Truth to Apparent Truth, producing an experience that jumps from Distorted Reality to Observed Reality.

It was quite apparent to my workshop participant, as soon as she stopped to think about it, that I would never harm her in any way, and that I was not her father. All she had to do to notice this was look at things more closely, and not simply accept her mind's first message about all that. This is what is meant by the oft-heard injunction: *Think Twice.*

So all you really have to do to change your thought about something is to Think Twice. When you are facing enormous change, and the fear that quite normally can be attached to it, many people will say to you, "Don't give it a second thought."

I'm telling you exactly the opposite.

I am a *precious occurrence,*
and I don't have long.
We, are a *precious occurrence.*
And as long as we think we have—
we don't have long.
Too much time is being wasted
running
from face to face
asking, "What is my name?"

If you don't yet know it
or if you've forgotten,
then become still, go within
and answer it.

—————

You, are a Precious Occurrence:
tell us your name.

—*'Precious Occurrence'* © 2008 Em Claire

14.

AND NOW, A
LIFE-ALTERING QUESTION

Okay, so we're clear now that changing your thought is simply a matter of thinking twice, of having a second thought about it, of noticing the moment.

Why don't we take a real-world example of something that could be happening to you right now and see how this process could work, okay?

First, I'd like to create a visual to go along with the *Notice the Moment* process, so that you can see exactly what we'll be doing. By now we all understand that there are three kinds of "reality." There is Distorted Reality (what you think is going on), Observed Reality (what you see right in front of you), and Ultimate Reality (what is "so" about what is going on, what is "so" about *why* it is going on—and what is "so" about *you*.)

We also know that these realities emerge from three brands of truth: the Imagined Truth, the Apparent Truth, and the Actual Truth.

Here is what that looks like charted out . . .

FROM ACTUAL
TRUTH EMERGES
ULTIMATE REALITY

FROM APPARENT TRUTH EMERGES
OBSERVED REALITY

FROM IMAGINED TRUTH EMERGES
DISTORTED REALITY

The small print within each of these levels denotes Points of Origin for your thought about what is happening in your life right now. The larger, bold print tells you where those starting points will lead you.

If you wish to change the experience of life that you are having right now, it is simply a matter of moving this starting point upward on the pyramid. It is a process of lifting your awareness as high as possible.

Now, because I don't know exactly what's going on in your life right now, we'll have to pretend. Let's say that you've just lost a relationship. Let's use that situation just for the sake of this illustration. You can take your own actual situation and apply to it the same formula we're going to use here.

Okay, now let's say that it was the other person in your relationship who ended it. The moment that person walked out the door for the last time, your mind started working.

First, your Human Brain searched all past data. It analyzed every other time in your life when you felt left, deserted, abandoned. It brought up all the data—Judged Data and Factual Data—from those prior experiences (including the time your mother left you in the crib and walked out of the room and you didn't know when she was coming back) and compared the information.

Now here is something you should know. It is the negatively Judged Past Data to which your mind will pay the most attention—because it is this data that your ego, which is the Here and Now operative of the mind, *does not want to experience again.*

So your brain looked at this negatively Judged Past Data, added it to the Present Data, and, mixing these data together, birthed a thought that created an emotion that it thinks *serves you*. Namely: deep sadness. This dropped you lower on the Pyramid of Being, moving you from Observed Reality to Distorted Reality. In short, you feel terrible.

As I've described, even if you've never, ever been rejected or abandoned before, *others have*, and so you will still have a basis in negatively Judged Past Data for creating thought and emotion. It will simply be *someone else's* negatively Judged Past Data—the cellular memories of your species, brought forward by your Reptilian Brain. From this you could, if you are not careful, produce an instinctive reaction.

And now, yet one more possibility, yet one more question: What if you *have* had a previous experience closely resembling your present experience, and your previous experience was *good?* What if the Judged Past Data that resembles Present Data holds good news? (Remember, not all Judged Past Data is negative data. Some of your previous experiences could have been judged to be quite positive.)

So now, what if your Judged Past Data tells you, *Don't worry. You've been through this before. Everything's going to be alright . . .* ? That would surely alter your here-and-now experience of the change that is presently occurring, yes? That would eliminate negative emotions, and produce a positive experience, right?

Well, it *could* do that . . . if we all *learned* from our "good" Judged Past Data. But there's something almost insidious that happens. The mind may bring up this positive data, but it will *pay little attention to it.* It's almost as if that good stuff *never even happened.*

Remember, your mind will always pay primary attention to "bad" past data, and scarce attention to "good" past data, *because this is the mind's job.* Your mind has been programmed to do this, in order to *ensure your safety and survival.*

In this sense it could be said that "good news is no news."

Are you getting this? Are you hearing this? This is really important, because it explains why in so many situations the first thing many people think about is *what could go wrong,* the first thing they focus on is *how bad things are,* the first thing they tell themselves is, *what a bummer!*

Wouldn't it be nice if this trend could be reversed? Wouldn't it be nice if in most situations the first thing most people think about is *what could go right,* the first thing they focus on is *how good things are*, and the first thing they tell themselves is *what an opportunity?*

Some people have a hard time with this. They don't understand how someone can see life as being so wonderful when they see life as being so difficult. My father told me from the time I was nine, "Son, get your head out of the clouds." And when friends see me downplaying or simply ignoring the possibility of bad outcomes, they have been known to say, "What, are you *out of your mind?*"

And my answer is, YES!!!

In order to experience life the way I am telling you that you can experience it, you've got to be OUT . . . OF . . . YOUR . . . MIND.

At least, for a while. At least until you have come to a really good understanding of how the mind works, of the Mechanics of the Mind, and of how you can change your truth in order to change your thought in order to change your emotion in order to change your experience in order to alter your reality of the event that is occurring in your life!

So, give yourself permission to Think Twice about what is occurring. Stay in the moment of Now, as Eckart Tolle would advise, and by so doing, raise your awareness from the Imagined Truth to the readily Apparent Truth.

If you can do that, you may come to a whole new conclusion about all that is going on. Let's see. Let's just see what happens when using this technique in our "make believe" example of your relationship having ended.

Looking at how you're feeling, you may be aware that you've created the following Distorted Reality:

I've been abandoned/Now I'm all alone again/This is really bad/I've been unjusted/I can't live without this person/I'll never be happy again/It was unfair the way it ended/I'm hurt and I will never forgive. . . .

Now—as you Think Twice—you are invited to consider an extraordinary question. One single question that can change your world. One inquiry that can change your emotion by changing your thought by changing the truth behind that thought.

Here is the Life Altering Question:

IS IT POSSIBLE THAT THE REALITY I AM EXPERIENCING IS NOT REAL?

At first this question might seem gratuitous and silly. You certainly know how you're feeling. You certainly know what is so. Your mind will argue with you if you try to squiggle out of the experience you're now having. *Open your eyes and look around!* it will scream. *You're abandoned! You're all alone again! That person's gone! GONE! You're going to be sad! You're going to be miserable! This is horrible!*

But if you have the courage to keep asking the Life Altering Question, eventually your mind will stop arguing with you and will at least look at all this again. It will Think Twice.

Quietly and without judgment, watch with simple curiosity and compassion (as Mary O'Malley would say) as your mind shouts inside your head: "Hey, don't give it a second thought! Don't give it a second thought!" because it *knows what's coming if you do.* Then gently insist that you *are* going to give it a second thought, you *are* going to take another look at it, before you carve your experience in stone.

Your mind will eventually cooperate. You can actually *train* your mind to cooperate. In this, you have to be like a master teaching an old dog new tricks. You have to be *a master mind.*

Now, if you have any questions on how this Life Altering Question process can work, you can check in with any of a number of people who are familiar with this material by jumping on the Internet at www.ChangingChange.net.

I hope you'll give yourself permission to do that, and to connect often at this interactive site, if it feels that this might be a good resource for you. And for now, how about if we take a little

Breathing Space

Breathe into what you've just read, then decide now if you want to go on right now, or rest with it for a while and meet with me here later.

If you're ready to go on, drop down to . . .

WHAT'S BEING WITNESSED?

Now let's run a dialogue here, shall we?

Let's look at what is right in front of you on this day of your life. (We're using, of course, our "pretend" example, since I can't talk directly with you right now . . . but I *could* if you and I were on one of our regularly scheduled group *conference calls.* . . .)

So let's look at this "pretend" example . . . but in our new way: let's limit the encounter with this moment to simply what is witnessed, rather than what is being felt about it. If you were in a workshop with me I would say, "Tell me, what happened here?"

And you might respond: "My partner just left me. I have been abandoned. I'm all alone again."

And I might say, "I understand that your partner just left you. This is something you have witnessed. This is Observed Reality. But have you been 'abandoned'? Are you 'all alone'? Is this what you have witnessed, or is this what you have *overlaid* on what you have witnessed . . . ?"

And you might respond, "I don't know what you mean. I'm not 'overlaying' anything. I have been abandoned. That is factual. I am all alone again. That's what's so!"

And here is how the dialogue might go from there . . .

"Really? What does 'abandoned' mean to you?"

"It means to be rejected, deserted, left. What the hell do you think it means?"

"By whom?"

"What?"

"Rejected, deserted, left . . . by whom?"

"By the one you love! By your partner! By the person you thought would be with you the rest of your life."

"Well, you've created a new meaning for that word in your imagination."

"What're you talking about?"

"Objectively, to be 'abandoned' means literally that: to be rejected, deserted, left . . . by *everyone*. To be *literally* 'all alone again.' Is that your Observed Reality? Is that what you observe about your situation right now?"

"You're playing with words here. You're just playing with words to make a point."

"No, *you are*. It is *you* who are playing with words, so that *you* can make a point with *you*. You are telling yourself something using words that you have loaded with emotion rather than witnessing."

"Man, you're losing me."

"No, *you're* losing you. You're losing you to your imagined self. You've embraced an Imagined Truth. But don't feel bad here. This is all quite normal. Just remain willing to change this experience if you can. Are you willing to change this experience?"

"I guess so."

"You guess so?"

"Okay, okay, I know so. I'm willing to change my experience."

"Good. Now tell me what you are able to witness today about your life. Are you abandoned?"

"My partner abandoned me, yes."

"Good. Who else abandoned you?"

Pause

"I'm sorry. Did you not hear my question?"

"I heard your question."

"Good. So who else abandoned you?"

"Nobody else."

"Nobody else?"

"No."

"So you have not actually been 'abandoned'—that is, left absolutely, completely, utterly alone. You have merely been left by one person."

"Yes. But that's enough."

"It's enough to feel sad, for sure. But is it enough to feel totally abandoned?"

"That's how I feel. I can't change how I feel."

"Sure you can. If you want to. You don't *have* to, but you can if you want to. Does having this experience make you feel good? Are you happy?"

"Of course not! You can *see* that I'm not happy."

"Well, if you're not happy, why do you keep giving yourself this experience?"

"I am not giving myself *anything*. This is *what's happening*."

"All right, let me ask you this. Are you all alone?"

Pause

"Not in the sense that you mean."

"Well, what other sense is there? What do the words 'all alone' mean?"

"I meant that I no longer have my life partner."

"I know that. But are you all alone? What is your witnessing? What do you see? Do you see any people in your life?"

"Of course."

"People who care?"

"Some of them do, I suppose."

"You suppose?"

"Okay, *okay*, some of them care. *Geez . . .*"

"So then you're not 'abandoned.' You're not 'all alone.' Right?"

"You're just trying to make me wrong about this. You're just trying to make me feel better about what's going on. You're not solving anything, you're just trying to make me look at every tiny detail so that you can prove your point, rather than listen to how I feel."

"Actually, I *am* listening to how you feel. And you're right, I *am* hoping to make you feel better. But I'm not doing it by *lying* to you. I'm not doing it by telling you something that isn't so. In fact, I'm trying to do it by telling you something that *is* so. I'm trying to get you to change the Point of Origin of your thought about all this. I'm inviting you to elevate from your Imagined Truth to your Apparent Truth, so that you can move from a Distorted Reality to the Observed Reality. I'm offering you an opportunity to see things from a different perspective. It is readily apparent to you that you are not abandoned and you are not 'alone again.' It is also apparent to you that your partner is no longer with you. You've mixed these two pieces of data and made them one. Can you see that?"

(Reluctantly) "Yes."

"Okay. Good. Let's start there, then. Now we're on our way. . . ."

(And the dialogue would go on, but we will not continue it here.)

That's a powerful dialogue even though I made it up, because, in a sense, I did not make it up. You see, I've gone through the "make believe" experience I used here. I'm not just remembering conversations that I've had with others in retreats and workshops. I'm remembering *my own inner dialogues.*

When I had the experience of being abandoned by a spouse (I came home in the middle of the day and found everything gone . . . a house empty of furniture and all of my wife's personal possessions), I had all of these same thoughts myself. I thought . . .

I've been abandoned . . . I'm all alone again . . . This is really bad . . . I've been unjusted . . . I can't live without her . . . I'll never be happy again . . . It was unfair the way it ended . . . I'm hurt and I'll never forgive her. . . .

All of these ideas have since been put to the test of time. They all seemed very real when I had them, reflecting my innermost truth. Yet I saw before too long that I was living my Imagined Truth, not the Apparent Truth. It became apparent to me over time that every one of these statements was false.

Every one.

So what does that tell you about the thoughts that you're having right now about *your* situation?

I am simply dreaming a way
to love Everyone within arm's reach.
I have help:
you, come toward me
with an aching in your eyes,
and a sadness leftover in your smiles.

———

In this new dream I am dreaming for me
I include *all of you*.
Do you want to know what *my* love is?
It is *your* love.
And all of us
Puppies
curling into

one

warm

heap.

—'Puppies' © 2006 Em Claire

15.

THE END OF PART ONE

So now we're approaching an important time in our conversation. We've looked closely—perhaps more closely than ever before—at the Mechanics of the Mind. Now that we understand how everything works, we've arrived at the moment when you have an opportunity to make a decision about the second, third, and fourth of the Nine Changes that you are being called to consider.

I see that you have already decided to make the First Change, to change your decision to "go it alone," otherwise you wouldn't still be with me.

The next three are . . .

Change #2: Change your choice of emotions
Change #3: Change your choice of thoughts
Change #4: Change your choice of truths

You can do this right now. You can use the Mechanics of the Mind to *change* your mind about the change that is taking place in your life right now.

Look right now at the emotion you've been feeling these past few days. Is it anger? It is fear? Is it grief? Is it frustration? Is it worry? Is it sadness? Is it disappointment, disillusionment?

Write down on a sheet of paper the emotions you have been feeling as a result of the change in your life circumstance. Finish the following sentence . . .

In the aftermath of what has happened. . . .

No, really, do this. This can help you. So go grab a piece of paper and do this. Describe in a few words the emotions you've been feeling and are feeling now. You might write, *I have been feeling . . . fearful.* Or you might write, *I have been feeling . . . sad.* Or you might write, *I have been feeling . . . angry.* Or all of the above.

Good.

Now write down the thoughts that you've had that have sponsored those emotions. Finish the following sentence . . .

When I contemplate all that has occurred and is occurring, I think that I . . .

. . . now complete the sentence. You might write, *I think that I . . . will never be happy again.* Or you might write, *I think that I . . . have been treated unfairly.* Or you might write, *I think that I . . . am in trouble here and am not going to be able to easily get out.* Or whatever you think when you contemplate the change in your life.

Good.

Now, write down the truth that you hold that sponsored those thoughts. Finish the following sentence . . .

My truth about this situation is that . . .

. . . now complete the sentence. You might write, *My truth about this situation is that . . . it is hurtful . . .* or . . . *it is dangerous . . .* or . . . *it cannot be solved . . .* or . . . *it. . . .*

Now, look at the Judged Past Data from which this truth emerges. See now if you can look past that Judged Past Data for just a moment, to the Factual Past Data. What is factual, without making a judgment one way or the other, about situations such as the present situation? What has your past told you, *factually*, about these situations?

Pretend that you are Mr. Spock on the starship *Enterprise*. Look at it logically. Looking at Past Data logically, and utterly without judgment, what do you see is true about the last two or three times this sort of thing has happened to you? Has it inflicted any kind of life-damaging injury, from which you have not been able to recover? Have you, in fact, recovered from a lot worse than this? Have, in some instances, things even turned out for the better when all was said and done? What is the *Factual* Past Data about all of this?

Now look to see . . . does this impact your truth about the Present Moment experience in any way? Can you *cause it* to impact your truth in any way? If you could, how would you cause it to affect your truth? Could you go so far as to create a brand new truth about what just happened?

Can you see yourself elevating from the Imagined Truth to the Apparent Truth?

This stuff works, my wonderful friend. This stuff works. But right now, listen to what your mind is telling you. Is it saying, "Yeah, yeah, for *you* it works. But for me, life is a constant struggle"—? Is that what your mind is saying right now? If not, *great.* But if it is, then start where Mary O'Malley, in her deep wisdom, would advise: curiosity and compassion. Just allow yourself to be curious about what your mind is saying, and have compassion for what you learn. Mary softly suggests asking these questions of yourself: What is the way through this? What am I really? What is asking to be seen? What do I need to say, do, or be that is for the highest good? What is needing my loving attention? What is the next step in my life?

"Bear witness." Watch gently where your mind is going, what your mind is doing. Do not make yourself "wrong" for it. Do not scold yourself or berate yourself, and above all, do not abandon yourself. Just be with yourself and be curious about yourself and ask yourself questions about yourself. And most of all, love yourself through all of it.

Stay with yourself, bring yourself to the present moment, maybe by just listening to your breath, maybe by looking at something in the room. Then quietly, softly, give yourself permission to make a new choice if you wish. Embrace a new truth.

We will conclude part 1 of this extraordinary exploration of how you can change everything . . . with a final insight about the Mechanics of the Mind:

TRUTH IS CREATED, IT IS NOT DISCOVERED.

God says, *"Lay the Hammer down."*
Which is really my own voice, make no mistake.
And it is your own voice, too.
So "Lay the Hammer down"
and bring your hand to your lips,
or lay it against your heart, whispering
"Sweet forgiveness,"
though there is nothing to forgive.
All we do is try to Love.
It appears as everything: anger, fear, and hurt of every kind.

But all we do is try to Love.

There is nothing to forgive
save, *lifting the Hammer again . . .*

—'*Lay the Hammer Down*' © 2007 Em Claire

PART TWO
The System of the Soul

And how knowing about that can help you create the changes in your life, rather than endure them

16.

THE ANSWER TO EVERYTHING

NOW WE LAUNCH INTO what I consider to be the most exciting portion of this or any other book.

Did I just say, "Or any other book?" Yes, I did. Because I don't think there's any book *ever written* that contains information more vital, more crucial, more critical, more important, more empowering, and more directly connected to your ability to experience life as you have always wished and hoped and aspired to experience it, than the information you are going to be given right now.

I hope you will make notes in the margins everywhere. I hope that the pages become ragged and dog-eared and thin from wear. If you're reading this electronically, I hope you will highlight every line and paragraph that shouts to you in your soul's own voice: *This is what you came here to hear.*

I want to tell you now about the System of the Soul.

The Mechanics of the Mind were just that: the mechanics, the interlocking, interacting devices in what I like to call "the engine of your experience." What we'll be examining now is the fuel. This is where the engine gets its power. And when we finish with the explorations in the second part of this book, you'll have everything you need to change everything when everything changes.

In a world that is constantly changing and a personal life that seems buffeted by major changes every time you turn around, it is important to understand how and why you experience change the way that you do, so that you can *change* your experience of change if you wish.

It is not easy to observe collapse, calamity, and catastrophe and remain at peace. Yet it can be done—and here, you and I are going to look at how.

We'll begin our exploration of the System of the Soul by announcing that you *have* a soul. This is not a "given" for all people. There are those who believe that humans are simply particular forms of life, that there is no "spirit" that lives inside of them. The discussion that follows presumes that the previous statement is mistaken. It further presumes the existence of what we might call an Oversoul—or what some people refer to as God.

These presumptions are based on more than blind faith. They are based on observation, logic, and the extrapolation of both.

We know from just a casual look at the Universe that energy exists. This energy appears to be at the core of every living thing—and, indeed, of *everything*, whether we normally refer to it as "living" or not.

For instance, to use our previous example, a rock.

A rock appears to be inert, and would not normally be categorized as a living organism in the usual use of those words. Yet if you define that which lives as that which *moves* according to an impeccable and precise design (which seems to suggest some level of *intelligence* at its core) that is clearly part of a larger and elegant *system*, then rocks are very much alive—for a close examination of rocks under a powerful magnifier will reveal a microcosm that is a virtual duplicate of the macrocosm.

It has not been lost on scientists and it should not be lost on you that telescopes and microscopes see the same thing: a *system* of particles or "balls" of energy, whirling at terrific speed around a core, or nucleus, the whole configuration of which is held together by some invisible yet obviously present and pervasive force.

Put another way, peer deeply into the sub-molecular structure of a rock (or *anything*) and you will see a small "universe." You will also see that *something is driving that universe*. This "something" cannot be seen. Its *effects* can be seen, but the energy itself that creates those effects is not visible to the naked eye.

Does this mean that energy does not exist? It does not.

All that can be seen is not all that is.

Now I come to tell you that what we have decided to call "the soul" is part of that which cannot be seen: an energy system that makes all things move and animates life. So, too, is what we have decided to call "God." In fact, God is *the system itself.*

God Is the Largest Manifestation of a System That Replicates Itself in Smaller and Smaller Versions through a Process That Empowers the System Itself to Exist and to Expand.

This is the System of the Soul, and it is impeccable. Its functioning is perfect. Its design is elegant. Its purpose is clear. Its power is immutable.

It can be no other way or the System itself would dis-integrate. That is, it would stop integrating itself, and thus, cease to be.

This would mean that God is in everything; that *life* is in everything. And this is true. And at a soul level, *we know this.* That is why we personify inanimate objects. We give our boats names and we fall in love with them. When our car won't start we pet it and say, "C'mon, Sweetheart, you can do it." *And the car starts.*

Mom makes a decision to redecorate and refurnish the living room and Dad says, "Fine, but my chair *stays.*" We find our baby blanket in an old trunk up in the attic and we hold it to our face and a tear comes to our eye and we *thank it* for all the comfort and love it gave us. *We thank the blanket.*

Do you think the soul is not clear that the Energy of Life is everywhere?

I tell you that *nothing* is not alive, *and the soul knows it.* The soul *sees itself in everything.* It knows our unity with all of life. It watches then, sadly, as the mind talks us out of this. Because the mind, you see, has only Past Data with which to come to its conclusions. Yet the soul goes beyond Past Data, to a place where time itself does not exist. The soul knows the Actual Truth, while the mind stops at the Apparent Truth.

Unless it does not.

And that is what the soul encourages the mind to do. It encourages the mind to not stop at the apparency of things. *Do not stop there*, it gently calls out. *Come with me, to a place you never even dreamed existed.*

All very interesting, you might say . . . *but what does this have to do with my life, and the changes that have taken place, and how I am going to deal with them?*

Ah, yes, there is that. . . .

(*Phew.*) Is this a good time for at least a tiny breath? Good. Let's *both* take a little

Breather right here

Let's take a moment to consider the implications of all that—and to consider that these implications *do* have to do with your life, with the changes that have taken place, and with how you are going to deal with them. Then . . .

. . . when, and only if, you're ready, drop down to . . .

THE ASTONISHING TRUTH ABOUT CHANGE

I consider that this entire conversation I am having with you will contain, in the end, two sentences that you will want to remember verbatim. I mean, really *remember.* As in, *never forget.* As in, tattooed on your left wrist, written in soap on your bathroom mirror, or magnetized to your refrigerator door.

These two utterances are paradigm-shifting and life changing. I call them . . .

1. The Life-Altering Question
2. The Answer to Everything

The Life-Altering Question marked the end of our exploration of the Mechanics of the Mind. Do you remember the question? Here it is again:

IS IT POSSIBLE THAT THE REALITY
I AM EXPERIENCING IS NOT REAL?

It is the soul that encourages this question.

And now comes *The Answer to Everything*. What I am about to tell you can make it possible for you to never have a negative experience of change again. This is the final piece of the puzzle. This is the lost key, the unknown combination, the secret of secrets. And while the Life-Altering Question was the culmination of the first part of this book, the Answer to Everything will be the launching point for the second.

Here it is . . .

ALL CHANGE IS FOR THE BETTER.

THERE IS NO SUCH THING AS
CHANGE FOR THE WORSE.

And *that* is what the energy system I have been describing has to do with you and your life. That is what *your soul* has to do with the changes that have taken place—and that *will* take place in the days and times of your future.

Life says for me to tell You This:
nothing needs fixing;
everything desires
a *Celebration.*
You were made to bend
so that you would find
all of the many miracles at your feet.
You were made to stretch
so that you would discover,
your own beautiful face of Heaven
just above
all that you think you must shoulder.
When I appeal to God to speak to me,
I'm feeling just as small and alone as you might be.
But this is when, for no particular reason at all,

I begin to
shine

—*'Shine'* © 2007 Em Claire

17.

THE FIFTH CHANGE

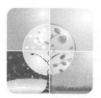

WHAT I HAVE JUST told you changes everything. No other piece of information is needed, no other data is required. The mind is now empowered to come to a whole new set of conclusions about Life.

Very early in this conversation I said that there were Nine Changes That Can Change Everything, but the truth is, the only one you need is . . .

CHANGE #5:
Change your idea about Change Itself

We have been seeing change as a disruption, as a break in the flow, as a shift in direction, as an alteration in the condition or circumstance of our lives. Especially with regard to what we view as unwelcome change, this has been our truth.

From this truth has emerged our thought, which has created our emotion, which has produced our experience, which has eventuated our reality.

I want you to think about what I just said. An *event* is what brings about our reality. Our reality is, in the literal sense, *eventuated.*

This is true *until we are out of our mind.* When we *leave* the mind and enter the realm of the soul, then it is no longer *events* that bring about our reality, but pure awareness.

From awareness emerges Actual Truth, while from events emerges, *at best,* Apparent Truth and, more usually, Imagined Truth. Thus, from events we travel into a Distorted Reality, while from awareness we move at last into the Ultimate Reality.

And what is it of which we become aware, that produces such a quantum shift in our overall experience? We become aware of the Actual Truth about Change Itself. We see that change is not a DISruption, but an Eruption. It is life erupting into fuller bloom. We see that change is not a break in the flow, it IS the flow. We see that change is not a shift in direction, it IS the direction itself in which all life moves. We see that change is not an alteration in the condition and circumstance of our lives, it IS the condition and circumstance of our lives.

In our expanded awareness we observe that without change, life itself would not be, for life is movement, and movement is change, by *definition.*

The question is not, therefore, whether life will contain change, but what kind of change life will contain.

And the answer to *that* question depends upon how you utilize the Mechanics of the Mind—and whether you integrate them with the System of the Soul, seeing these as two handles of the same Larger Tool.

Let us, then, examine this System of the Soul, even as we examined the Mechanics of the Mind, and let us begin where we began . . . with a definition of the Soul itself.

The soul is energy. It is the energy of life itself, animating life itself. Life energizes and animates life itself through the process of life itself. It is a self-feeding, self-sustaining *system.*

Those last few words are vitally important to remember. Life is a *self-sustaining system.* It never ends, but sustains itself eternally. How? By *adapting.* Why? So that it can remain forever *functional.* When it can no longer function in a particular way, it adapts. By its adaptation does it render itself sustainable.

Life is making its adaptations in every moment. It is always changing. The question is not whether life is always changing, but why? Life is always changing in order to remain always sustainable. Thus, every change that ever occurs is *change for the better.*

This new idea about change that I'm inviting you to embrace, when put on a more personal level, reads like this:

All change is for your own good.

Most of us experience this—after the fact.

Most of us have experienced events which we have called, when they were happening, the worst moments of our lives, only to find, as time went by, that what occurred was *one of the best things that ever happened to us.*

The fact is that this is true of *everything* that has ever happened to us, but we do not know this, we cannot accept this, because some things *have* turned out for the worst—*according to our definition.* Yet our definition is warped, constrained as it is by the Mechanics of the Mind, *and their inherent limitations.*

The mind may very well know all about what has gone before, but it does not know *why.* The mind may very well hold all of life's Past Data, but it does not hold all of life's information (which is another thing altogether). The mind may very well contain knowledge, but it does not contain wisdom.

Wisdom lies outside the mind. Wisdom resides within the soul.

That is why we need to hold both handles of this magnificent tool of creation that I shall now call by its proper name: YOU.

Let me make something very clear. "Facts" and "awareness" are not the same thing. We can know all the facts about gravity, but if we do not have an awareness of why gravity works, *we know nothing.* We can know all the facts about electricity, and we can even use electricity, but if we have no awareness of what electricity *is* and of *why* it works, *we know nothing.* We can know all the facts about light, and we can even use light, but if we have no awareness of what light *is* and of *why* it works, *we know nothing.*

Likewise, we can know all the facts about change, but if we have no awareness of what change *is* and of *why* it occurs, *we know nothing.*

For instance, we may not know that . . .

NOTHING CHANGES FOR THE WORSE. EVERYTHING ONLY CHANGES FOR THE BETTER.

That's a pretty big statement, and I understand if it's hard for you to believe. Yet it is true. Let's step back a little from this enormous idea and give it some basis in physics. Yes, I said *physics.*

I have been saying that the mind is a mechanism. Now I want to say, so is life. All of *life* is a mechanism, and like all mechanisms, life operates on energy. Unlike most other mechanisms, life *is* the energy on which life operates. That is, it feeds on itself.

And so, stars implode and entire star systems disappear into black holes; and so, earthquakes and tornadoes and hurricanes ravage the earth; and so, big fish consume little fish; and so, humans are born, live their lives, and die—ashes to ashes, dust to dust. Yet the energy of none of this—*none of it*—disappears, but merely changes form. Energy is never, and can never be, lost; it can only be transformed.

It is through the transformation of energy that light is produced. It is through the transformation of energy that heat is produced. It is through the transformation of energy that electricity is produced. It is through the transformation of energy that gravity is produced. It is through the transformation of energy that *everything* is produced, including Life itself.

Energy acts upon itself. The transformation of energy produces energy in formation. Energy is *life's information.* Life is always in formation. It is forever forming itself into something it was not before it became what it is. It is through the becoming that life breathes life into Life itself. In simple terms, this is called change.

Yes, there's that word again . . . *change.*

That is what life is all about. Life nourishes life through the process of life itself, in which life changes its form a hundred million times in the blink of an eye, a *million* million times in seconds, a *billion* million times in a minute, and more times than Time itself can count in the time that has passed since counting began.

Change for the *worse* is literally impossible within the expression of energy that we call Life. That's because Life itself can fundamentally alter itself in only one direction: the direction that evolution requires; the direction that expansion demands, the direction that keeps it flourishing. Things can only change for the better, things can only improve, because "improvement" is the *only Nature of God.*

Put another way, God has no intention of doing Itself in.

Life is God's way of proving Itself to Itself. The process by which It does this is called *Improvement.*

But wait a minute! Who even says there *is* a "God"?

I do. But I am not using the word God as many other people do. I do not use the word to denote or describe a huge Super Being existing somewhere in the cosmos, exhibiting proclivities and tendencies, needs and desires, frustrations and emotions identical to those of humans. I am not talking about an Entity Divine who has needs that must be fulfilled *or else,* who presumably has a temper (or, at least, a determination to punish those who disobey), and who also has, presumably, a penis, and, presumably, fair skin, and, presumably, no wife, but One Son.

This is not the God I am referring to when I use the word "God."

I am referring to the Source of Supreme Intelligence manifesting itself as the Pure Energy that we call Life itself. I am referring to the Largest Manifestation of a System That Replicates Itself in Smaller and Smaller Versions through a

Process That Empowers the System Itself to Exist and to Expand. I am talking about the biggest undifferentiated stem cell in existence, from which life in all its forms emerges.

Indeed, in my understanding and experience the words "God" and "Life" are interchangeable, and in this equation evolution is the constant. It is the ever-present mandate of Life itself. It is the continual, the unending adjustment, adaptation, and alteration of All That Is. No adjustment, adaptation, or alteration *contracts* Life, but can only *expand* it. No adjustment, adaptation, or alteration *diminishes* Life, but can only *enhance* it.

Life evolves to higher and higher levels of complexity. Life could not *devolve* if it wanted to. It is incapable of doing that.

Now, it is true that life can *look like* it is devolving. Changes can *look like* they are not "for the better." But, in fact, change can only be for the better or it would not occur. All spiritual masters know this. That is why all spiritual masters teach, each in their own articulation . . .

. . . judge not by appearances.

Life is eternally functional, adaptable, and sustainable. These are the Basic Principles of Life, and they cannot be violated or rendered in any way inoperable, or Life would cease to be.

All of this becomes much easier for people to comprehend with my simple substitution of the word God for the word Life. Suddenly, everything is made clear. God is eternally Functional, Adaptable, and Sustainable. These are the Basic Principles of God, and they cannot be violated or rendered in any way inoperable, or God would cease to be.

When human beings embrace the extraordinary idea presented here, the process of change will be seen for what it is: the ultimate expression of Divinity Itself, sustaining Itself through adaptations that render Itself eternally magnificent.

Change is an announcement of Life's intention to go on. Change is the fundamental impulse of Life itself.

Again I want to tell you that I don't think that a lot of people see it this way. If they saw it this way they would heed the injunction of Christ, and "be not afraid." Yet "ye of little faith" *are* afraid. Thus it was that Franklin Roosevelt was moved to say, "We have nothing to fear but fear itself."

I'm going to take that one step further. I'm going to say . . . *We have nothing to change but Change itself.*

Today I awakened quieter than God
and stretched my Self toward the sky
to caress the celestial bodies
with the

Body of God

—————————

All night long
The Sun awaited my eyes.
And now that they are upon Her
She rises, as Divined as every siren
every muse
every

Body of God.

Even Ocean sways and rocks
in gentle wait for me to wake

even Moon

even Sky

even Silence

Even Silence awaits the Awakening of my voice
that will tenderly kiss Its body of sounds

still

in the Body of God.

—*'The Body of God'* © 2009 Em Claire

18.

THE SIXTH CHANGE

I HOPE YOU HAVE considered The Fifth Change carefully, and that, given the information and the insights you've received here, you feel that you can go ahead and embrace it, along with Changes One, Two, Three, and Four.

I want to say that if there were one change on my list of nine that could do the work of all the others, Change #5 would be it. This is a change that can change the way change is experienced even as change is taking place. Isn't that a change you would like to make?

Sure it is. We'd *all* like to make a change like that at times such as the moment you are experiencing right now.

Now I know that the way *you'd* like to change things is to change the fact that anything changed at all! It may look as if you can be happy again only if you can change *what happened.* But here's the news: that's not going to make you happy.

If keeping things the way they were was going to keep things happy, what has just happened wouldn't have happened.

Now you might be able to put in place yet *another* change, following the change that has just occurred, which could return things to something *resembling* the way they were before, but they will never again be exactly the same—and you would not want them to be. Always remember this: you cannot change what's been changed, because that's already in the past, but you *can* change the future, and that's where your power lies.

Your decision will be, do I want to change the future so that it duplicates my past? Or do I want to change the future so radically that it looks *nothing at all* like my past?

In order to consider this carefully, you should be aware that change does not occur in a vacuum. Change does not take place in the universe for no reason. Change is not a random act. *Change is an announcement that something is not working.*

The change that has occurred in your life has happened because disharmony was present. When disharmony is present, life becomes dysfunctional—and that condition violates the first of the Basic Principles of Life (Life Is Functional, Adaptable, and Sustainable) and invokes the second.

Okay . . . now you might say, "If all things happen for the better . . . I mean, if that is really *true* . . . then someone needs to tell me what in blazes God has in mind, because *things sure don't look any better to me!*"

I know that I'll be hearing that a lot during the Changing Everything Workshop that we're presenting in satellite TV "web casts" around the world, and in our twice-annual live, in-person retreats. And this leads us to . . .

CHANGE #6:
Change your idea about why Change occurs

Even if you accept that all change happens for the better, you do not know why this new circumstance, situation, or condition *is* better. You don't understand the nature of the improvement. That's because the improvement may not have to do with exterior conditions, but with interior conditions. What you are not seeing is *why* change occurs—and who is causing it. When you see this and embrace it as your living truth, once again everything in your day-to-day experience will . . . well . . . *change*.

So here comes another Actual Truth. Get ready.

Are you ready?

This is a tough one, so take a breath. Okay, here it comes . . .

Change occurs because you want it to occur.

Everything that changes changes at your direction.

Whoa, *that* sure doesn't seem true! Why in the world would you *want* to have happen what has just happened? *No one in their right mind would choose that!*

Are you saying this (or screaming it) inside your head right now?

Well, if you are you would be right. No one in their right mind *would* choose something like this. The mind does not make these choices. The soul does.

All of which gets us to the *agenda* of the soul. First we established that you *have* a soul, yes? Now we need to look at *why.* Why do you have a soul? What's its purpose? What's its function? When you understand this (or freshly remember it), it will be very clear to you why you would choose the change you have chosen just now.

Your soul's agenda flows serenely with the larger energy of life itself. Life's energy always moves toward synergy, harmony, glorious expression, and expansion. It seeks an experience of itself, in fullness.

When I add my own human language to this understanding I find myself saying that life's energy always moves in the direction of what I call "love." Love of self, love of others, and love of life.

Your own individual energy moves in the same direction. Your soul and the "soul of the universe" desire, seek, and produce at all times the same thing. It is when your *mind* gets in the way that it seems as though it is not producing this, that something terrible has happened, and that you're going in the wrong direction.

I'm going to use an example now from Christian doctrine to illustrate what I am saying here. The New Testament tells us that Jesus went with his disciples to a garden in a place called Gethsemane. There, he asked his followers to sit and wait for him and to pray. He, too, he said, was going to go off to pray, but by himself.

And then, being alone, he felt a great heaviness come upon him, almost to the point where he could die. And he knew what lay ahead. And he called out to God, "Father! You can do anything! If there is any way that this can happen, remove this cup from my lips. . . . "

Here Jesus' mind had gotten involved, and he wanted a change of direction in the way things were going. But immediately his vibration was raised, through the sheer power of his will. "Yet not my will, but thine," he said. And with those words his soul returned to alignment with the soul of the universe—or, if you please, with God.

There is but One Soul, yet there are many expressions. These individuated aspects of the One Soul seek synergy, harmony, glorious expression, and expansion. This is another way of saying that life in all its forms seeks the very same thing that Life itself seeks. How could it be any other way?

Yet the soul and the mind are two different things. The "life form" that you have taken has both a soul and a mind (as well as a body), and it is in this triune totality that it fully equips itself to do what you came here—to physical life—to do.

The job of the mind is to make sure that the body—your physical instrument, or tool—is kept safe, so that you may use it to do what you came here to do. The job of the soul is to make sure that the mind always knows what you came here to do, and does not get caught up in its own make-believe world.

It is like getting caught up in a virtual reality on the Internet. I'm sure you must know that there are now entire "worlds" on the Internet into which you may enter, claim an identity, and live an entire "life"—growing up, finding love, creating a career, buying a home, having a family, experiencing success and becoming rich (or not) . . . you can actually produce an entire experience of life in these virtual realities, interacting with others, entering into legal agreements—it's all really quite detailed, sophisticated, and complex. *And none of it is real.* Obviously, not a single bit of it is really happening to You. It is only happening to the "you" that You created in that make-believe world.

To your soul, physical life on the earth is very much the same thing. The trick is not to get "lost" in the make-believe world of your mind, but to *use* your body and your mind to do what your soul came here to do.

We are all doing that right now, but some people are doing it consciously and some are doing it unconsciously. That is, *without knowing what they are doing.*

Now I know that some of this may be starting to sound a little bit far out, so maybe it would be a good time to just take a little rest here and just kind of "be with" all that's been said. Try not to judge it or evaluate it. Just rest with it and let it be just what it is: merely an idea, one person's concept; something for you to consider. Okay? So, for now, would you like to

Take a break?

And when you're ready, pick up the chapter at . . .

A QUESTION OF BALANCE

What happened to Jesus in the Garden of Gethsemane is what happens to all of us. I love the fact that this story is in the

Bible for that very reason. It gives us all hope if we know that even Jesus was having to deal with the balancing of his mind and his soul as part of the process by which he had the fullest experience of himself.

That's what we're talking about here in this conversation. I'm wanting to assist you in seeing that life is not exactly what you may think it is, and that there is a *reason* that things are happening the way they are happening, and that you are not a *victim* to this reason, but, rather, that you are *at cause in the matter.*

This idea would be difficult for you to embrace unless you had a clear understanding of your true identity; of who you really are and why you are here on the earth in physical form and what life is really and truly all about.

Absent such an understanding, none of life will make much sense. *With* such an understanding, *all of it* makes sense. And when it makes sense to you, you no longer have to suffer the pain and the frustration that you have known in your life so far. Changes can come along right and left (and they will), and they will not discombobulate you, or draw you into anger and sadness. You will have changed the way Change itself is experienced—because you will have understood everything there is to understand *about* Change, including that . . .

All change is change for the better.
Change occurs because you want it to occur.

The mind rejects such notions, but the soul shouts them to high heaven. This is because the soul knows what the mind cannot comprehend. And *this* is because the mind comes from Past Data, while the soul comes from EverMoment.

EverMoment is my name for the moment of now. It is the only moment that ever is. There is no moment other than EverMoment—although we have created the illusion that there is. We've created this illusion for a reason.

The mind has broken down EverMoment into bits of information about life, called *data*. It has categorized these data (because that is its *job*). Your mind takes in data from what it experiences as something it calls "now" and stores it in memory according to certain criteria. This is pretty effective and pretty efficient—except for one thing. Your mind has a very narrow view of "now." Its perspective is extraordinarily limited. *This is by design.* If your mind took in all the data about everything all at once, and tried to *process* it all at once, you would be able to make little sense out of it. That is because too much data is almost worse than no data at all. (Anyone who has gone into a restaurant to find a menu with 101 items knows this experience exactly.)

In order to consider the data of EverMoment and make it useful (given what it is that you are here to do, which we are coming to), that data must be considered *one piece at a time.*

Now this can be done rapidly—indeed, *very* rapidly—but it still must be done sequentially. That is, one item at a time. And even in this, all items may not be considered, but some must be separated out, so that each item may be considered in and of itself. It is for this reason that the mind voluntarily assumes a limited perspective.

You do this in your own life. If a time comes when you feel you are "on overwhelm," you may well say in aggravation to those around you, "Wait a minute, wait a minute! *One thing at a time!*" Your mind does this automatically. Thus, its perspective is not one in which The Whole of things may be considered, but only a portion of The Whole. Again, this is quite by design.

Your mind is a marvelous mechanism, as I have explained, AND . . . it is important that you understand exactly how it works, so that it may work *for* you and not *against* you.

Now . . . the fact that your mind holds a limited perspective does not mean that *you do.* This would only be true if you were only your mind. But you are *more than that.* And *this* is the crux of the whole point that I have come into your life right now to make.

You are *more* than your mind. You are also a soul. Indeed, this is the biggest part of you. I don't want you to think that I am accusing you now of being small-minded (heh-heh), but, in fact, your mind is the smallest aspect of your individuated Self. Its perspective (one more time, for emphasis . . .) is very, very limited. The impact of this limitation is going to be made clear to you very, very shortly.

The soul, on the other hand, is not limited in its perception. It knows everything, sees everything, understands everything, and *has* everything that the living entity you are could possible wish to have. It has these things because it *is* these things. It has love because it *is* love. It has peace because it *is* peace. It has harmony because it *is* harmony. It has synergy because it *is* synergy. It has glorious expression because it *is* glorious expression. It has all these things and more. There is only one thing it does not have. It does not have the *experience* of them.

That is where the rest of you comes in.

Now we are getting down to the nub of it. Now we are getting down to the System of the Soul, and how it works.

The soul operates on a system of Synergistic Energy eXchange—or what we have abbreviated as S.E.X. All of life operates on such a system and is created by it. When energy is transferred, it is transformed. It then becomes energy in formation. This energy information is broken down by the mind, as I have already described, into bits of data.

Now, in this conversation I have created the term EverMoment because I needed a word that is larger than Now. EverMoment contains more than what *the mind* refers to as Now. EverMoment contains what *the soul* calls Now—which in mind-terms includes "yesterday," "today," and "tomorrow."

Now, the mind can gather all of the data that is presenting itself to us "today." And it can recall in an instant all of the data is has stored about "yesterday." But the one thing the mind cannot do is gather data about what it calls "tomorrow." If it did, it would see that yesterday, today, and tomorrow are really Always. The mind's inability to see the "future" as part of "now" is why we say it has a very limited perspective.

The System of the Soul is a system by which the individuated aspect of Divinity known as You can step back from what is Apparently True (based on the limited perspective of the mind) to see what is Actually True (based on the limitless viewpoint of the soul) for a period brief enough to not "unravel" the mind, but just long enough to open the mind to a larger perspective.

We have all had such "flashes" of insight, such fleeting moments of total awareness, such glimpses of The All. During such moments a veil is lifted and we move quite easily from Apparent Truth to Actual Truth. The purpose of such insta-parency is to allow the mind to know that there is *more data* out there than it may be aware of; unknown and unexperienced information regarding life.

In truth, it is not really unknown and unexperienced, it is merely forgotten. The function of the soul is to help you remember all that you already know—but not too much, too fast, or it will "blow your mind." That would do no good at all, because you need both your mind *and* your soul to move through life in a way that satisfies your reason for coming here.

By allowing your mind to remember bits of Actual Truth that you have not experienced in this lifetime (and therefore do not have in your memory), the soul assists you when you are having any here-and-now experience that you are not understanding and enjoying. It gives you the ability to elevate your experience from Distorted Reality to Observed Reality—and then upward still, to Ultimate Reality.

You should know that even Observed Reality is a very wonderful place to be. Most humans do not get there very often, and fewer manage to remain there very long. Living in the Observed Reality is, it turns out, a high state of being. In this state, we distort nothing, but see everything for exactly what it is in human terms. This can remove us, a great deal of the time, from fear.

The movement from Imagined Reality to Observed Reality is a big one. The shift from Observed Reality to Ultimate Reality is usually a much shorter step. When your consciousness resides in Ultimate Reality, the limited perspective of your mind expands beyond belief.

I mean that literally. It expands beyond what you now believe, to a place where belief is no longer necessary, having been replaced by absolute knowing. How long you can hold on to this perspective and still operate in your day-to-day life in the way that you must if you are to meet your life's objective is the question. Those who do are "in this world, but not of it." We see them as masters. We acknowledge them as avatars. We seek to follow their example. Yet until now we have not even known what they were doing, much less how they were doing it. That's what this conversation is all about.

Things will be different now, you know.
Not the snows, blanketing mountains in June.
Not, "The frost came early" or "stayed late."
The kind of different
that stains the soul.
That leaves an Innocent dusted
with
every new color of God.

—————

Once you have seen deeply
and been deeply seen
you know that
nothing
has ever, ever been as it seemed.
That Your own reflection is
every Christ, every Goddess, every Buddha, and Brahmin—
put simply: the *Everyone's Heart.*

—*'Things Will Be Different Now'* © 2008 Em Claire

19.

THE ETERNAL
JOURNEY OF THE SOUL

IN ORDER FOR YOU to change your idea about why change occurs you will have to change your idea about who you are, where you are, why you are where you are, and what you are trying to do here.

These are the ideas we have been circling around in this conversation for a while now. They are what I have called Life's Four Fundamental Questions. Most people have never asked themselves these questions, much less answered them. I believe it is vitally important that you do so if you want to live a happy, fulfilling life, because the answer to these questions could dramatically alter your perspective.

It is also important to note that there are no single answers to these questions that are "right." That is, however anyone answers these questions, their responses are "right." In a world where "reality" is created and not observed, it is by definition true that *everyone is right.*

I said a number of pretty important things there. May I review and expand on them just a little?

I said that there are four basic questions that I believe all people must ask themselves if they are to have a meaningful life. I said that it doesn't matter how they answer them, their lives will become more meaningful for having done so. I implied that this is because reality is created and not observed. And finally, I said that everyone is right about everything.

These statements all have to do with one thing: perspective. And in the matter of changing everything when everything changes, perspective is the key.

That is, I think, the largest message of this book. Indeed, it may be its only message. In truth, the entire conversation we have been having could be reduced to these three words:

PERSPECTIVE IS EVERYTHING

If this is true, then if we want to change everything about the way we experience change in our lives the primary question becomes, *How do we create, and then change, our perspective?* This book has been an attempt to answer that question, first by exploring the Mechanics of the Mind, and now by looking deeply at the System of the Soul—*and the journey upon which the soul has embarked.*

For too long, matters of the mind and matters of the soul have been separated. Many, many people have felt that the world of our physical reality is one thing and the world of our spiritual reality is another—something like the individual person's version of the separation of church and state. Yet in a world where everything is changing so rapidly all around us, we can no longer afford such a piecemeal approach to dealing with life.

I have said here: when everything changes, change everything. I have also said that if we are to negotiate our rapidly changing future, we must change the way we experience Change itself.

I am now saying that in order for us to do that, we must adopt an integrative approach to the living of our lives. That is, we must understand—and *function from the understanding*—that our spiritual vibrancy, insight, and experience are no less important to our here-and-now on-the-ground expression of life than are our mental vibrancy, insight, and experience; that spiritual and mental are not, in fact, separated, but act co-jointly as what I call the Total Being That Is You; and that the only reason we do not experience this (if, indeed, we do not) is that we *do not know anything about it.* No one has taken the time, in our upbringing or in our later life, to tell us what is really going on here.

Hold it. That's a sweeping indictment and, in fact, it is not true. Many people have taken the time to explain life's intricacies to humanity. It is I—and perhaps you—who have not taken the time to listen. Yet now we are both listening, because the events of our lives are demanding that we do so. We are being driven by the day-to-day circumstances of our existence to seek answers and approaches that can make life more functional, more joyful, more rewarding, and, frankly, just make more sense. And so we come to a new, contemporary explanation such as this. I come to it and you come to it, and we are both welcome here. It is, lit-erally, *well* that we have come here.

This is, perhaps, a good time for me to tell you how it is that I have come here, to this information, so that you may have a larger context within which to consider what I have been sharing with you.

Perhaps you are aware that I have written a series of books under the title *Conversations with God*. These texts were based on my experience of having received *data* from a source *beyond my mind.*

I have called this source "God" because I believe there is a God, and that when She communicates with us, He does so in many ways, not the least of which is in direct conversation/inspiration/explanation/revelation.

The experience I had was so extraordinary that I wrote about it in a trio of books. And then I found that I could not stop writing, because the flow of what was "coming through" was not stopping, and I did not want to keep it all to myself. So, six more books followed the original trilogy. Six of those nine books made *The New York Times* bestseller list, the first remaining on that list for 135 weeks.

I'm not boasting here, I'm sharing this with you to let you know that nearly eight million people have seen this material, in thirty-seven different languages—meaning that an enormous number of human beings are opening to alternate ways of conceptualizing life and experiencing and expressing and *creating* their current reality. You see, the *CwG* material is not intended to open people to *my* truth, it is intended to open them to their own. I'm also telling you this so that you can come to a realization that, no, you are not "crazy" for taking a serious look at life in the way we are doing here (multi-millions of others have done it), and no, you do not have to wade through the changes and the challenges in your life all by yourself.

Now, fifteen years after my first dramatic experience of God as a real presence in my life, the flashes of insight keep coming, the moments of awareness endlessly arrive, the glimpses of The All continue to materialize. And what these glimpses show me is that the glimpses themselves are being offered to everyone.

Everyone.

It isn't that there is one of us who is more "privileged" or more "special" or more "holy" or more "able" than everyone else to access wisdom and to be provided a direct connection with the Divine. There is no Chosen One. We are *all* able, we are *all* chosen, and the question is not, to whom does God talk? The question is, *who listens?*

Having said that, I want to very quickly add here that just because one is listening does not mean one is hearing everything in fullness; just because one is having a conversation with God all the time does not mean one is completely *understanding* all the time, or interpreting *without error* all the time, the information to which one has gained access.

In my own case I have never claimed and would never assert that the messages I have published are infallible or "God's own truth." I can only declare that I have done my best to transmit them as I have received them through my imperfect filter, and that even in the imperfect state in which I have understood and expressed them, they have brought me great benefit and an expanded awareness and a wonderfully enhanced experience of life. Yet as I share them with the public I invite—indeed, encourage—everyone to place them in the For What It's Worth Department, and to turn inward to heed their own voice of awareness.

Indeed, if my conversations with God experience has done anything, I hope that it has produced the outcome that more and more people everywhere are *going within* to the Source of Wisdom and Truth that lies inside each of us.

With that as the context, I want to invite you now to look at some more "stuff" for the For What It's Worth Department—namely, Life's Four Fundamental Questions. I consider this the most important exploration I ever took.

But wait. It feels like a good time to

Take a breath, yes?

When you're ready, pick up this chapter at . . .

YOUR ANSWERS, PLEASE . . . ?

My life changed direction radically when I answered these questions:

1. Who I am?
2. Where am I?
3. Why am I where I am?
4. What am I doing here?

Actually, I did not answer these questions. *I asked them.* I went inside to the Source Within and posed these inquiries. Here are the answers I received:

1. You are an Individuation of Divinity. There is only One Thing, and all things are part of the One Thing That Is. Life is

God, expressing Itself. You are a part of Life, therefore, you are a part of God. The only way this could not be true would be if Life and God were somehow separate. Such a thing is impossible.

2. You are in the Realm of the Physical, which is part of what you have called Heaven. The sadness is that you do not think that you are in heaven, and so your Imagined Reality is that you have to *get there.* In fact, there is nothing you have to do, nothing you have to be, and nowhere you have to go to experience paradise. Merely look upward on a starry night, or outward over a foaming ocean, or toward the skyline at dusk or dawn, or, for that matter, into the eyes of your beloved. You are in heaven, and you are calling it something else, and you are acting as if it were something else, and so, of course, you have *created it* as something else.

The Realm of the Physical is one of three realms in the tri-une reality that you have called by various names, including heaven, paradise, nirvana, the afterlife, the Kingdom of God, etc. The other two realms are: The Realm of the Spiritual and the Realm of the Spirisical (which is the point between the two). Think of this as a *figure 8* on its side.

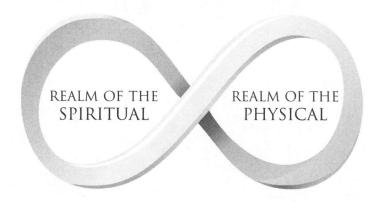

REALM OF THE
SPIRITUAL

REALM OF THE
PHYSICAL

The Total Being That Is You is on an eternal journey from the Realm of the Spiritual to the Realm of the Physical and back again. The Realm of the Spirisical is at the cross point between the two.

(This illustration was given to me as a simple visualization to assist my mind in holding data that cannot actually be visualized, it being outside the human experience. A figure 8 on its side is—not by coincidence—the international symbol for *infinity*.)

In the Realm of the Spiritual everything exists in absolute form, whereas in the Realm of the Physical things exist in relative form. In the Realm of the Spiritual all things are absolutely what they are. In the Realm of the Physical a thing is what it is relative to other things that are *not* what it is.

Big and *Small*, therefore, do not exist in the Realm of the Spiritual, but only in the Realm of the Physical. *Here* and *There*, likewise, do not exist in the Realm of the Spiritual, but only in the Realm of the Physical. As well, *Now* and *Then*, *Fast* and *Slow*, *Male* and *Female*, *Up* and *Down*, *Light* and *Dark*, *Good* and *Evil*, *Love* and *Fear* . . . none of these things exist in the Realm of the Spiritual, but only in the Realm of the Physical.

In the Realm of the Spiritual it is always *Here* and *Now*, and there is only *Light* and *Love*. Thus, we could rename these realms, calling them . . .

REALM OF THE
ABSOLUTE

REALM OF THE
RELATIVE

In the Realm of the Absolute you know absolutely everything, and you know it absolutely. Yet you cannot experience what you know, because there is nothing else. For instance, you can *know* that are you Love, but you cannot experience yourself *as* Love, because there is nothing that is *not* Love.

You can *know* yourself as Light, but you cannot *experience* yourself as Light, because there is nothing else *but* the Light.

You can know yourself as Good, but you cannot *experience* yourself as Good, because *Evil* does not exist.

The formula is this:

IN THE ABSENCE OF
THAT WHICH YOU ARE NOT
THAT WHICH YOU ARE
IS NOT

That is, it cannot be made real in your experience. You can know yourself *conceptually*, but you cannot know yourself *experientially*. You can *conceive* of yourself in a particular way, but you cannot *experience* yourself *being that way* because there is nothing else *but That Which You Are.*

Here, then, is the Conundrum of God: How can God experience Itself? *By not being God.*

Unless It was not God (that is, not the Totality of Itself), God could *understand* Itself to be magnificent, but God could not *experience* Itself *being that.* Again . . . why? Because there was nothing else *but* "magnificence" in the Realm of the Absolute. God could understand Itself to be enormous, endless, and timeless, yet these concepts had no meaning since there was nothing that was *not* "enormous," "endless," and "timeless." God could understand Itself to be All Powerful, yet power could not be experienced in an environment in which there was nothing *but* absolute power in equal measure.

Since God wished to Know Itself *experientially* as well as conceptually, God created a place in the Kingdom (or, if you will, in Ultimate Reality) where all that God Is could be *experienced* as well as *known*.

God did this by *dividing Itself up* into a million ka-jillion different parts, or Aspects of Itself, with each of the Parts created in different sizes and shapes, colors and textures, speeds and sounds, and levels of visibility and invisibility. Then any Part of The Whole (that is, any Individuated Aspect of Divinity) could look back on The Whole from which It emerged and say, "Oh, my God, how magnificent Thou art!" All it would take would be for that particular Aspect to have sufficient consciousness (self-awareness) to do so.

And so, after dividing Itself up into a million ka-jillion individual parts, God merely had to imbue some of those parts with sufficient consciousness to recognize (that is, re-cognize, or "know again") Divinity when it was looking right at It. (Not all human beings have risen to that level of consciousness.) God put into place a *system* by which Individuations of Itself *could* rise to such a level, and that system was called evolution.

This is the *System of the Soul.*

You now know about the Mechanics of the Mind and the System of the Soul. There is more to learn, however, about this System—which you will do presently.

We see, then, that the Realm of the Absolute (also known as the Realm of Spirituality) is where KNOWING everything takes place, and that the Realm of the Relative (also known as the Realm of the Physical) is where EXPERIENCING everything takes place. It might be said, then, that souls come to the earth in order to gain *a world of experience.*

We therefore can give the realms in the Kingdom of God yet another name . . .

THE REALM OF
KNOWING

THE REALM OF
EXPERIENCING

Whichever of the three labels you choose, you will be correct. These names are interchangeable, and the various names have been given to us so that we might look at Ultimate Reality in whatever way makes the most sense to us, thus allowing us to comprehend the incomprehensible.

But it was said that there is a *third realm* in the Kingdom (or in Ultimate Reality), do you remember? We said, at first, that there was the Realm of the Spiritual, the Realm of the Physical, and, at the cross point between them, the Realm of the Spirisical.

Spirisical is, of course, a word that I simply made up, because there is no word currently in human language to indicate what this realm is all about. This realm is not a place where the other two realms combine, but rather, a space from which the other two realms *emerge.* It is difficult to describe in human words the exact nature of this realm, but if we drop down to our third set of labels we perhaps can get close.

In our third set of labels we called the realms of the Kingdom of God the Realm of Knowing and the Realm of Experiencing. The third realm, the realm at the cross point, might then be called the Realm of Being. Situated at the cross point of the figure 8, this is what you experience when you *cross over.* That is, when you move from the Realm of the Physical to the Realm of the Spiritual.

This Middle Realm is where *pure being* occurs.

Yes? Are you getting it? Are you beginning to see a Larger Picture?

Now you might ask, "What is that? What is pure being about?" My answer would be that in the space of pure being you both know *and* experience Who You Really Are. This knowing and experiencing *simultaneously* is the experience for which God yearns. It is God's greatest joy. It is the wonder of Divinity, fully known and fully expressed! It is nirvana. It is bliss. It is heaven.

Yet heaven is not limited to this. The *whole process* is heaven, and the wonder of the process is that the Total Being That You Are can be in nirvana, bliss, and absolute joyfulness at any point in the process. The cross point was simply created in order to *ensure* that each Individuated Aspect of Divinity would never be lost from the feeling, but would be *guaranteed* nirvana, bliss, and absolute joyfulness.

This is what you experience when you "cross over" at the moment of your "death" (which does not really exist) and at the moment of your rebirth (your next re-entry into the Realm of the Physical).

You see, the Ultimate Reality is actually a circle. One rounded whole. The energy of life travels in this circle, through all eternity. It is the cycle of life. In the beginning, God WAS this circle, in place AS the circle, complete. When God individuated Itself, it sent the individual Aspects of Divinity on a journey around the circle. So fast did these infinitesimal bits and pieces of God travel that they seemed to be everywhere all the time. Like a tire spinning so fast that it seems like a solid circle not moving at all, so, too, the cycle of life replicated the Always Everywhere-ness of God by seeming to create a solid where there were really moving parts.

By dividing itself up into a million ka-jillion such parts, each part could look back upon The Whole and suddenly have a context within which to consider the magnificence of The Whole—and thus, to *know God.* Yet how could each of the Individuated Aspects also know *Itself* as God? That was the question! While each Individuation raced through the cycle of life, how would it know what it really was? Seeing the rest of It, would it know that It WAS the rest of it, in singular part?

To know this, the Individuated Aspect would have to be able to experience the utter joy that was now God's—for God, through the cycle of life, could now know and experience Itself *simultaneously*—and that was bliss, indeed. Yet how could it be guaranteed that *each Individuation* would move into this bliss as well?

Ah, there's the twist. And so, in order to ensure this, the Circle that is God twisted itself to form a figure 8, reasoning that if at *one point* both sides of the circle could touch, then the

Totality of Being God could at that point be known and experienced by every one of God's Individuations!!!

Do you get it? Do you see it now???

Each Individuated Aspect of Divinity, traveling on its journey through the endless cycle of life, may both know and experience Itself as Who It Really Is at any place on that cycle. *You* can do this now, in any moment of your present lifetime. Others have done it. Masters have done it. Masters are called "masters" because they have *known themselves as God.*

Some of them have even *called* themselves that. Yet when you call yourself Divine as you travel with those who do not know themselves as that, they are liable to be offended by you. They may even crucify you. They will surely disassociate from you, *even as they long to be and experience what you are demonstrating.*

Do you get it? Do you see it now???

When you reach the Cross Over Point on your current cycle of life, you will know the bliss and the joy of Being the Totality of Who You Are. And you will do a great deal more. You will *decide* how you wish to expand that. You will *choose* what you *next* wish to know, experience, and Be—for life is a continual process of recreating the Self.

This is what God is up to!

God is doing this through the reformation and the transformation of every aspect of Itself, *one aspect at a time.* You are, in fact, doing exactly that during every passage from realm to realm on the eternal Journey of the Soul. You just may not know it. When you *do* know it—when you are aware of who are you, where you are, and why you are here—you will then have evolved in consciousness sufficiently to do the work of God, and not just what *appears* to be the task of being human.

This is what I have meant all along when I spoke to you earlier of the difference between the Apparent Truth and the Actual Truth. All of which brings us to the answers to Fundamental Questions #3 and #4:

3. You are where you are because in the Realm of the Spiritual you can know absolutely who you are, but you cannot experience that in relative terms. And so, you venture into the Realm of the Physical so that you may gain a "world of experience."

4. What you are doing in the Realm of the Physical is using the tools and devices (which include your own body, by the way) that are only available in this realm to bring you the *experience* of what you have decided, in the Realm of the Spirisical, that you wish to be, and that you then come to *know* your Self as in the Realm of the Spiritual.

Creation and Re-creation of Self is a three-step process: Choosing, Knowing, Experiencing. You cannot experience what you do not know, and you cannot know what you do not choose to know. It is really quite simple, and the model is elegant in its design.

This is the System of the Soul. This is who you are, where you are, why you are where you are, and what you are doing here.

I Am That I Am
and
so much more:
the Light, the Sound, the Living of God on the Ground.

I could show you every feather in the Wing.
Every color and hue.
Every Beautiful thing.
But
I Am That I Am
wants to
LOVE
Whoever has not yet had it.
Whatever has not yet known it.
However Life's not yet done it.

———

There is still so much Loving,
yet to be found,
just
Living God on the Ground.

—'I Am That I Am' © 2007 Em Claire

20.

THE POWER OF PERSPECTIVE

EVERYTHING I HAVE just told you is, of course, only my perspective. True, I gained this perspective from my conversation with God, but that makes it no more valid than any other person's perspective. Your conversation while visiting the place of wisdom within you may produce an entirely different perspective.

How is this possible if there is only One Truth? Is it possible because there is *not* only One Truth. All truth is subjective. The truth is not discovered, it is created. It is not observed, it is *produced*.

Quantum physics tells us that nothing that is observed is unaffected by the observer. That statement, from *science*, holds an enormous and powerful insight. It means that everyone sees a different truth, because everyone is creating what they see.

Wow.

Hold *that* in your awareness for a while. Wow.

In fact, let me say it again, so that you really get it. *Science*—not *spirituality*—tells us that:

NOTHING THAT IS OBSERVED
IS UNAFFECTED BY THE OBSERVER

Put another way: *The place from which you are looking determines what you see.*

It seems that God is creating God's Experience of Godliness . . . *one Individuation at a time.* Thus, there is no "right answer" to Life's Four Fundamental Questions. There is only the answer you give.

Having said this, let me add that I firmly believe that *some* answer *must* be given if you seek to live a life that is nourishing, rewarding, *taking you someplace*, and providing you with the equipment to get there by changing any aspect of your life that you no longer find joyful—including your experience of Change itself.

One of the beauties of life is that not only do we not all have to give the same answers to life's most important questions, we also do not have to stick with the answers that we have given. We can *change our mind* anytime that we wish!

If, when everything changes, you wish to change everything, the first thing you may wish to change is your idea about *why change occurs.* This is Change #6, and it is a life-altering, reality-shifting occurrence.

My idea is that change occurs because of who you are and why you are here.

I am saying that change occurs because you want it to occur. I am saying that you want it to occur because you are continually choosing the perfect people, places, and conditions with which to experience what you next seek to experience as you move forward in the process of the evolution of your soul.

I am saying that your life on earth is about much more than you may have ever dreamt. It is about deciding, creating, expressing, and experiencing Who You Really Are (as opposed to who you think you are), and it is about recreating yourself anew in every golden moment of Now in the next grandest version of the greatest vision ever you held about that.

I am saying that you have the power to do this precisely *because* of Who You Are. I am saying that, given that you are an Individuated Aspect of Divinity Itself, you have the ability to create your own experience of life and, thus, your own reality.

I am saying that you have an opportunity to do this every day of your life by using the Mechanism of the Mind to decide how you wish to respond to, and thus experience, every single thing that happens to you, while using the System of the Soul to choose a perspective from which to respond.

I am saying that *perspective is everything.*

I am saying that only the System of the Soul can be wholly effective in creating your perspective, because only your soul knows all that is so about This Moment Now, and about *all* the moments in time, because only the soul *spans* all the moments of time.

I am saying that the mind alone cannot view the Present Moment with such an expanded awareness, because the mind is limited to Past Data as it analyzes the Present Moment, and try as it might, it cannot get out of that box—but that you can *put into that box* the New Data of a larger perspective.

(You are doing that right now, in the reading of this book.)

I am saying that it is the job of the soul to provide the mind with this additional data, and that the part of you that is Divine is shameless! It will use any device, any tool, any event, any person, *anything it has to*, to wake you up, and only the soul knows what aspect of Divinity the Present Moment was designed to bring you an opportunity to express.

I am saying that if you use the mind alone, without the collaboration of the soul, to respond to daily events, you will cut the Line of Causality in half, severely limiting your ability to respond in a way that reveals to you Who You Really Are—to say nothing of your ability to step into *who you next wish to be*.

You will remember I've said that the mind has a very limited perspective. This is, I have hoped to make clear, quite by design. It is not a "handicap," but an elegant schematic, allowing a limited physical device (the brain) to comprehend the unlimited metaphysical expression that is Ultimate Reality.

Your limited mind does this one piece of data at a time. If it took in all the data about all of life all of the time, it would not process the data accurately, and you would no doubt be judged to be, in the clinical sense, out of your mind. Thus, in order to render the mind a useful tool, the Total Being That Is You has made sure that all that the Total Being knows and understands is fed to the mind in bits.

Okay, that's a lot to absorb. Before you are given any more "bits" of data right *now*, perhaps we might stop here, if only for a moment, and

Take a breath

Good. Now, when you're ready, let's go on to . . .

ENLARGING THE LINE OF CAUSALITY

I have been referring here to a new identity, and I wonder if you've caught that. I have referred a number of times to the Total Being That Is You as if it were an entity unto itself—and, in a sense, it is. And this is something that you should know, because this awareness is at the *core* of how to change everything when everything changes.

The Total Being That Is You is *both* the mind *and* the soul—as well as your *body*. It is the three-part being that you are now, have always been, and always will be. Body, Mind, and Spirit is the triumvirate. It is the Holy Trinity. It is You, with a capital Y.

Now here is another bit of data about how to change everything: The process of life has nothing to do with learning.

I know, I know . . . everyone says that "life is a school." Well, maybe it is, but it is not a school where you are trying to learn something you do not know. It is a school where you are given an opportunity to remember what you *already* know.

In the strictest sense you cannot learn anything at all, because you came here (to physical life) already knowing everything you needed to know to do what you came here to do. So your mind is about the task of creating experiences that allow you to "remember" what you came here to remember, so that you can experience what you came here to experience—and the part of your Total Being that I am naming your soul is co-creating this experience with your mind and your body by joining the mind in calling forth the perfect people, places, and conditions that will allow you to do what you came to physical life to do: namely, evolve.

You soul also works in conjunction with the body and the mind to let you know that it is doing this, and how. It serves as guide, direction giver, helper, assistant, and as your Connector with the Divine.

Your soul is your connection with God.

God is your soul, writ large. Thus, your soul is a Small Part of God connected with the Totality of God. It knows exactly where your mind needs to go next in order to next remember what it needs to remember as your Total Being continues on the path that we have called evolution.

Why do you suppose you're reading this book?

Earlier I said that I would explore with you how the limited perspective of the mind impacts your reality, and why it is therefore so very wise to spend some time *each day* in communion with your soul, so that the soul and the mind may make the journey of daily life together.

Now you know. Now you understand. It is vital to spend some time each day connecting with your soul in some way in order to *use* the System of the Soul, for the soul brings to the mind a Larger Perspective, and perspective has great power. It is, in fact, the most powerful element in the process of reality creation.

I wonder if you really heard that; if it had any impact on you. We've been saying so much, so fast, that sometimes it's easy to miss the nuance of things. Let me say it again.

Perspective is the most powerful element in the process of reality creation.

Yes, yes, I've already made that point a number of times now. I am reminded of that old, old song that contained the lyric line: *Kiss me once and kiss me twice, then kiss me once again.*

It's been a long, long time. I want to change that to the Song of the Soul:

Tell me once and tell me twice, then tell me once again. It's been a long, long time.

It's been a long time since you were fully aware of Who and Why you are. It's been a long time since you were in that place of Absolute Knowing. Years and years of Earth time have passed. And so I am telling you things here once, and twice, and then once again. For the time has come for you to fully remember. That is, for you to become *a member once again* of the Body of God. This is a process of re-*membering*.

You do this by raising your consciousness, thus expanding your awareness and waking up your mind, one bit of data at a time. How? Keep reading. I'm going to tell you. But first, here is that last bit of data, being presented to you for the third time:

Perspective is everything.

Now since the mind has a very *limited* perspective, it will not benefit you to insist on using the mind *and only the mind* to understand life. Nevertheless, that is what most people do. Very, very few people commune daily with their soul. When thinking deeply about life, *they leave their soul out of it.* Yet it is the soul, not the mind, that holds the Larger Perspective you need to fully comprehend life and, thus, to change it.

The soul tells us that it is perspective that creates perception, perception that creates belief, belief that creates behavior, behavior that creates events, events that create data, data that create truth, truth that creates thought, thought that creates emotion, emotion that creates experience, and experience that creates reality.

Remember earlier when I referred to the Line of Causality? I presented it as this:

event+data+truth+thought+emotion=experience=reality

Now I want to tell you that I was presenting to you then *only part of the line.* I did not want to dump into the space too much data at once. I know that when *I* received this data, I could not have received it all in one download. I mean, I wouldn't have "gotten" it. I would have said, *"Too much, too much! Too much too soon. I'm outta here."*

The One Soul knew that, and so I came to full awareness about the Line of Causality in two parts, and I thought I'd offer it to you in the same way. I hope that's all right. . . .

So . . . here is more of the data about that Line of Causality. The line is larger, and looks like this:

perspective+perception+belief+behavior+event+
data+truth+thought+emotion=experience=reality

I trust you can read that. What this longer, complete Line of Causality shows us is what comes *before the event.*

What causes *events* in our lives are the *behaviors* of our lives. And what causes the behaviors of our lives are the *beliefs* of our lives. And what causes the beliefs of our lives are the *per-ceptions* of our lives. And what causes the perceptions of our lives are the *perspectives* of our lives.

And this is where the soul comes in.

It is the *soul* that can enlarge the perspective of the mind beyond the limitations of currently held data. The soul is able to do this because of the soul's level of awareness. The soul's awareness emerges from the soul's level of consciousness. The soul's consciousness emerges from the soul's State of Being.

That is, One with Everything, across all time and in every place. This is the Actual Truth and the Ultimate Reality.

You can experience this State of Being even while in your body, by any process you may wish to use (there are many) that allows you to sidestep your mind temporarily, placing you in immediate contact with your soul.

Now we are going to present the Line of Causality as a *vertical* line—for that is what it really is. When you finish with this exploration you will understand everything about causality . . . *from top to bottom.*

Here is how it all works, here is the flow . . .

BEING

CONSCIOUSNESS

AWARENESS

PERSPECTIVE

PERCEPTION

BELIEF

BEHAVIOR

EVENT

DATA

TRUTH

THOUGHT

EMOTION

EXPERIENCE

REALITY

From pure Being flows Consciousness, from Consciousness flows Awareness, from Awareness flows Perspective, from Perspective flows Perception, from Perception flows Belief, from

Belief flows Behavior, from Behavior flows Events, from Events flow Data, from Data flow Truth, from Truth flows Thought, from Thought flows Emotion, from Emotion flows Experience, from Experience flows Reality.

Of course, there are no straight lines in the Universe. Everything curves in on itself. Therefore, this line is all a circle, and if there is no interruption in this circular path, Being leads to Ultimate Reality, because that is the reality from which it emerges.

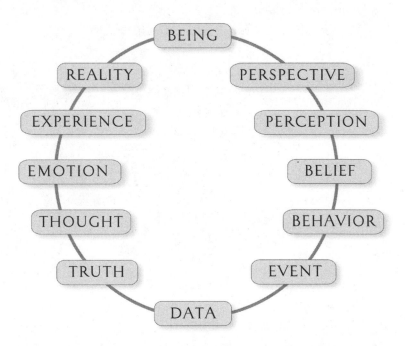

Everything takes place in the physical world in a "moment" that we call "time." A bunch of these moments can be charted on a clock. It may help you to think of your soul as moving through this imaginary moment, working "around the clock" to bring you the richest experience of Who You Really Are.

Each "hour" on the cosmic clock you move one step away from Being, in order that you may return there, knowing/experiencing it again. By the process described in the steps you see on this Time Clock, you create and recreate yourself anew as "time" passes. Finally, you reach "the eleventh hour." This is when the way in which you "passed the time of day" plays its effect.

Okay now, follow the "clock" with me now . . . if you do not remember the perspective with which you began (that is, the perspective of the soul), you could hold a perception that produces a belief that results in a behavior that manifests an event that creates data that leads to a truth that generates a thought that outpours an emotion that culminates in an experience that causes you to wind up at the eleventh hour in a Distorted Reality.

And so the question of the hour (so to speak) is: how can you remember the perspective with which you began? The answer is: by using the System of the Soul. The Mechanics of the Mind will never get you there, for the simple reason that information about where you began is not stored in the mind.

The mind only holds the data that it has gathered since it was biochemically mature enough to begin data-gathering activities. Therefore, the only stored data in the possession of your mind is data about your body's physical adventure (both before and after birth, I might add). Any other data that may burst upon your present-moment awareness comes either from your body's cells (its cellular memory, described earlier) or from your *soul*—which knows and understands everything.

That is why I advise you to go within. For it is as *Conversations with God* says: "if you do not go within, you go without." I have been in touch with my own soul (as have many, many people the world over, using a wide variety of techniques; later I will offer you a detailed description of ways in which you may do this) and it has been made very clear to me that there is only One Soul, of which my soul is a part, and that the System of the Soul is elegantly simple.

This is the source from which I learned the reason that things change. To repeat:

Change occurs because you want it to occur. Everything that changes, changes at your direction. You want it to occur because you are continually choosing the perfect people, places, and conditions with which to experience what you next seek to experience as you move forward in the process of the evolution of your soul.

How does change move evolution forward? Your *response* to the changes occurring in your life is your answer to that question.

So this is how it all works:

Life is always functional. When any facet of it (any person, place, or thing) begins to skirt the edge of functionality, life detects this shift of energy at once and puts into place an adaptation. This adaptation assures that life remains sustainable. As life sustains itself through its new, changed form, life becomes functional once again.

The small part of life (God) that is You *chooses* for things to change when the changes that are already (and always) occurring threaten to produce instability in the system. Your soul can detect the onset of system instability long before it can have any negative effect. *That is its job.*

Sensing the onset of instability—like a child's top whose spinning is slowing down—the soul awakens the mind, which then actively co-creates with the soul (and with all other energies in the system) whatever change (adaptation) will keep things spinning at optimum velocity.

All of this is why I have said, Life is a process that informs life about life through the process of Life Itself.

You are who you say you are, and your experience is what you say it is.

(This may be one of the greatest secrets of life.)

Change #6 is about changing your idea about why change occurs. It calls upon you to embrace a new notion: that life's changes are neither arbitrary nor without rhyme or reason, but, rather, are very sophisticated adjustments in a very sophisticated system—the System of the Soul.

You see, your soul is here on a mission. It did not just suddenly find itself here, nor did it place itself here without purpose or reason, function or intent. It knows exactly what it is doing, and your mind and your body and the physical life all around you are the tools with which it (and every other soul) is doing that.

Life conspires to bless us with an
unrelenting Grace.
Who among us has not been touched by this generous hand,
freeing us,
one
or many layers
at a time?
You are the lucky one
who has known annihilation
and then absorption
back into the Love
we seek.
And it is *you* who knows
that even as the soul-cry rends your very chest,
the whole of the Universe
shakes
with Love.
In this place of All
there is at long, long last
no place
left
to fall.

—'Unrelenting Grace' © 2006 Em Claire

21.

THE SEVENTH CHANGE

THIS BRINGS US TO the next change in our list of nine—the change that moves the process of your soul's evolution forward by focusing not only on what is happening right now, but also on what will be happening tomorrow.

The System of the Soul is, you will remember, a system of energies. These energies impact upon themselves. That is, their effect is circular. As it has so often been said: *what goes around comes around.*

This is another way of saying that the Line of Causality is like that clock we used as an analogy earlier. It is the System of the Soul and the Mechanics of the Mind, *linked.*

If you do not know they are linked, you will pay attention to one and not the other. You will walk around with your head in the clouds all the time (as my father worried that I was doing), completely detached from your physical reality, or you will walk about with your nose to the grindstone all the time (as I did for a while when I overcompensated in response to my father), completely detached from your spiritual reality.

Either way, you will create and experience, at the eleventh hour, a Distorted Reality, not the Ultimate Reality. You will find it difficult to jump even to the Observed Reality—which is too bad, because even Observed Reality is a very special place to be. The majority of people do not get there very often, and fewer people can manage to remain there very long. So living in the Observed Reality is a very high state of being. In this state, we distort nothing, but see everything for exactly what it is in human terms (if not in spiritual terms). You are, essentially, pulled out of your "drama" and away from your Story. This can, in turn, remove you a great deal of the time from fear.

The process that I have created and use in my Changing Everything Workshop gives people a chance to do that. It offers participants an opportunity to move from Distorted Reality to Observed Reality in a very short period of time. I like to say that it can take you from tears to laughter in seven minutes. (I have seen this happen in our workshops!)

We go farther, then. We take participants from laughter to the *joy of awareness*—which is a different level of happiness altogether. It is not just a place where you move *away* from fear, but where you actually transform it, changing the very meaning of the word. We use this acronym:

F-E-A-R = Feeling Excited And Ready.

The person who is coming from Actual Truth, and therefore living on an even higher plane in the realm of Ultimate Reality, is always in such a space, is always "feeling excited and ready," because that person does not even see the same things that a person living in the Observed Reality sees—for the simple reason that the person living in Ultimate Reality is looking at everything from an entirely different perspective . . . from that *third* reality that modern clinical psychology *doesn't even acknowledge exists.*

Do you remember this? *The place from which you are looking determines what you see.* Indeed, it does. And so the trick is to live as an integrated whole, with all *three* parts of the Totality of Your Being—Body, Mind, and Spirit—creating, expressing, and fulfilling your current notion of Who You Are and Who You Choose To Be—and with you gathering that notion not from your Imagined Truth, not from the Apparent Truth, but from the third level of truth: the Actual Truth.

By moving to the Actual Truth as your Point of Origin, you can use the Mechanics of the Mind to *transform any moment.* And you access this Actual Truth by using the System of the Soul to *change your perspective.*

Is this real? Can this really happen? Those are fair questions. You may now be asking those questions yourself. I have come (or, more accurately, you have brought me to you) to tell you this: yes, it is real. This is how the soul and the mind work together in a synergistic process that allows the Total Being That Is You to do what you came here to do; to use this life as you were intended to use it.

So far I have invited you to do six things. I've invited you to change your decision to "go it alone," to change your choice of emotions, to change your choice of thoughts, to change your choice of truths, to change your idea about Change Itself, and to change your idea about why Change occurs.

Now, with this background, I'm going to invite you to make a stupendous change, a humongous change, a mountainous, gigantic, gargantuan change. I'm inviting you to make

CHANGE #7:
Change your idea about future Change

It may not have yet occurred to you that the System of the Soul can be applied to future change as well as presently experienced change, but it can. In fact, this is where it has its greatest power, because it can systematically change not only this moment, but *your entire life*.

I have said now a number of times that change occurs because you want it to occur. You want it to occur because you are continually choosing the perfect people, places, and conditions with which to experience what you next seek to experience as you move forward in the process of the evolution of your soul. Now you may not feel that the change that is now occurring has been caused by you, but it has been, at a very high metaphysical level, through the process of synergistic energy exchange. In simple terms: thought in action. What some have called the Law of Attraction.

Yet why would you attract something to you that you do not experience as being very welcome? Because it is only in your *mind* that it does not seem welcome. In your soul it is very clear that the change now presenting itself is your simple and intuitive assertion of the Principles of Life (life is eternally functional, adaptable, and sustainable).

But, you may ask, how is what is happening now actually "good" for me?

Well, you can experience that in two ways. You can either wait long enough for the passage of time to show that to you (which it inevitably will), or you can go to the place of knowing that right now.

That place is your soul, not your mind. Your soul will show you now what your mind will show you later. Later, as life unravels itself, you will see that *everything that's ever happened to you has happened for the better.*

What a statement! What a God we must have!

Now I know that it is compelling (and important) to bring this up right now: what about the unthinkable plight of those people who have endured unimaginable suffering in their lives?

I know, I know . . . and I agree that it is very, very difficult for the limited perspective of the human mind to hold such suffering as acceptable, purposeful, or intentional on the part of the soul. Yet *Conversations with God* has been very clear on this point. It says there are no victims and there are no villains in this world. Everything that happens is happening for the highest evolutionary purpose—and it is notable that sometimes a soul reincarnates at a time and for a purpose that *serves the agenda of another.*

Such a statement could be made about the man named Siddhartha Gautama, who came to be called the Buddha. It could also be made about Moses, who led his people out of the desert and into the promised land. It could also be made about Jesus Christ, whose message has likewise impacted the world entire. It could also be made about Muhammad ibn Abdullah, bless his holy name, a diplomat, merchant, philosopher, orator, legislator, reformer, military general, and, according to Muslim belief, an agent of divine action; a messenger and prophet of *Allah*. It could also be said of many other masters and avatars and saints, some known and some not known, but easily recognizable by their actions, by what they have given and what they have sacrificed in order to serve the sacred and holy agenda of others.

(This idea, this concept, is described in beautiful terms easy enough for a child to understand—indeed, *written* for a child—in the wonderful book, *The Little Soul and the Sun*, a children's literature bestseller that emerged from the messages in *Conversations with God.*)

Into this final category falls a multitude of contemporary figures, or what might be termed *latter-day* saints . . . which include, of course, more than the members of a particular religion. People such as Mother Teresa, Paramahansa Yogananda, Mahatma Ghandi, Martin Luther King Jr., and even persons still closer to our present history, such as Nelson Mandela, who lived in captivity for nearly thirty years and emerged from jail to forgive his jailors—and to ask a country to do so as well.

What kind of man is this? A man who has listened to his soul, not just to his mind, and who has thus *recontextualized his experience* by adopting a perspective that opened him to a perception that produced a belief that impacted his behavior in a way that produced events that created data for the mind of man that resulted in a truth from which emerged thoughts that generated emotions that stirred an entire world, creating an experience that elevated humanity's reality forever.

And let me make it clear that such modern saints are not limited to persons who lead movements or nations. Your own mother may have been such a saint, or your father. Or both. Ordinary people doing extraordinary things have often sacrificed in order to serve the sacred and holy agenda of others. We cannot guess what that agenda may be, but we can see that it takes modern saints to carry it out. Ronald Cotton is such a person. He simply led an ordinary life—much of it behind bars.

You see, Ronald was found guilty of raping Jennifer Thompson one night in 1984 in Burlington, North Carolina. I heard about Ronald and Jennifer in a story broadcast by CBS News on *60 minutes*. The story recounted how Jennifer identified Ronald as her rapist, and how he spent eleven years in prison for the offense. There was only one problem. He didn't do it. He said he didn't do it, but nobody believed him. After all, as *60 Minutes* showed, Jennifer Thompson had identified him, and she was certain when she did so that she had found the right man.

But in 1995 new DNA evidence revealed that another man was the rapist. After eleven years in prison for a crime he did not commit, Ronald Cotton was set free. The story made all the news and was highlighted in March 2009 on *60 Minutes*. Today Ronald Cotton and Jennifer Thompson are friends. In fact, they have written a book together with writer Erin Torneo, *Picking Cotton*, in which they share their story. Most fascinatingly, they have become good friends. They speak regularly on the phone, and they travel together to bring to light the many problems with eyewitness evidence.

As dramatically recounted on *60 Minutes*, the first time Ron Cotton saw Jennifer Thompson after being released from prison, she told him with tears streaming down her face, "If I spent every second of every minute of every hour for the rest of my life telling you how sorry I am, it wouldn't come close to how my heart feels. I am so sorry." She said he just reached out, took her hand, and said, "I forgive you."

Cotton said that when he spoke quietly with the woman in a church where she asked him to meet with her, he told her, "I don't want you to look over your shoulder. I just want us to be happy and move on in life."

What kind of a man looks into the face of a person who falsely accused him of a crime that sent him to prison for over a decade and forgives in an instant?

Well, human beings, it turns out, are capable of such extraordinary responses to life when they expand their viewpoint beyond the limits of the mind to the perspective of the soul. They may not even know, consciously, that they are doing this (or they may not call it that), but they are making a choice about life and how they are doing to live it, and I suggest that this choice comes from a place deep within, far past the reaches of the mind.

When we use the System of the Soul (our higher knowing) *with* the Mechanics of the Mind, we have combined the two most powerful tools with which human beings are endowed. Knowing that everything that has ever happened to you has happened in some way for your own higher good and fastest evolution is very, very empowering. For it means that everything that is *going* to happen to you in the future is, likewise, for your own good.

This radically alters your idea about future change. You no longer have to fear it. And by not fearing it you take control of it, because you now feel free to take the actions and decisions that are most desirous, rather than always opting for those that are most cautious.

It is desire that ignites the engine of creation, not caution. Never, never caution. Always, always *desire*.

Look to see what you most desire in your life, then ride that feeling all the way to creation. If you do this you are using what has been called the Law of Attraction. In simple terms: thought in action. At a very high metaphysical level: the process of synergistic energy exchange.

Everything is energy. In this field of energy, like attracts like. What you think, you create. Yet what you believe is what you think, and what you perceive is what you believe—and all of your perceptions depend on your perspective . . . AND . . .

It is your current reality that creates your next perspective.

It is a circle. I know you have already heard all of this . . . but *I want you to really "get it."* If you step out of a Distorted Reality you could carry that distortion into your next perspective, skipping right over the place of Pure Being from which the soul's perspective emerges. This will affect your next perception, which will affect your next belief, which will affect your next behavior, which will affect your next event, and so on around the clock of your life . . . to the creation of your Next-Moment-Reality.

This is not good. Life is not going to go well if your Distorted Reality is so strong and feels so "real" that its energy affects your next perspective. That's why you are urged to get in touch with your soul, which rests between your last reality and your next perspective (at "twelve o'clock high" on life's

Time Clock). What the soul brings to this process that the mind cannot is that *enlarged perspective* I keep talking about.

Once you have gained that new perspective, once you have made that *New* Data part of your mind's *Past* Data, you can think a new thought about tomorrow, and how you want it to be. You do not have to come from worry or anxiety or negativity or any less than joyful vision of your future—no matter *how* "bad" you think today has been! Knowing that all things turn out for the best, that all outcomes are perfect for your evolution, gives you extraordinary confidence in tomorrow. *And that's where your power lies.*

Okay, enough for a while. I'm going to invite you now to just

Put the book down for a bit

Give yourself a chance to take all of that in. Read the notes you've placed in the margin. (You *have* been taking notes, haven't you . . . ?) Maybe do a little writing in your journal. (You *are* keeping a journal, yes?) Then . . .

. . . when you feel refreshed, please go on to . . .

YOUR NEW IDEA ABOUT TOMORROW

What I'm saying here is that life is an energy that feeds on itself. Life produces more life through the process of life, and life's energy duplicates itself. What I'm saying here is that thinking in a positive way about a present event not only changes our present experience of that event, but sets into motion energies that create future events. What I'm saying here is that an extraordinary life emerges from a change in your idea about future change—#7 on our list.

What you project, you produce. What you conclude, you create. And all that stuff.

"All that stuff" is what spiritual teachers of every stripe and color, of every persuasion and belief, have been sharing with humankind since time began. All spiritual teachers say the same thing. Don't you think that's a bit unusual? All religions teach the same doctrine. Don't you find that interesting? On this particular subject, on the question of how life works and what makes the world go 'round, every dogma agrees: *As you believe, so will it be done unto you.*

James Allen wrote an extraordinary little tract on this subject, titled *As a Man Thinketh.* I read this more than thirty years ago and it changed my life.

The James Allen website [self-improvement-ebooks.com] says that this mystical author (1864-1912) wrote in his own powerful words what the Buddha taught: All that we are is the result of what we have thought. Allen's text has it this way: "As a man thinketh in his heart, so is he."

Allen's message "is one of hope even in the midst of confusion. Yes, he says, humanity surges with uncontrolled passion, is tumultuous with ungoverned grief, is blown about by anxiety and doubt. Only the wise man, only he whose thoughts are controlled and purified, makes the winds and the storms of the soul obey him," the website says.

This is, of course, exactly what I have been telling you here. Again I notice, it is what *all* spiritual teachers and writers have said forever and ever. In a striking affirmation of the very book you are now reading, James Allen wrote one hundred years ago:

"Tempest-tossed souls, wherever you may be, under what-soever conditions you may live, know this—in the ocean of life the isles of blessedness are smiling and the sunny shore of your ideal awaits your coming."

Thus, says the self-improvement-ebooks.com website, "Allen teaches two essential truths: today we are where our thoughts have taken us, and we are the architect—for better or worse—of our futures."

My grown sons have a way of dealing with whatever is going on in their life. No matter what happens they say, simply: "It's all good."

You can't make a scheduled lunch date? "It's all good." The car gets grumpy and won't start? "It's all good." I like that. I like that a lot. What a perspective! What a great starting point! *That's how you create a wonderful tomorrow!*

You create from a new Point of Origin about *today!* The opportunity that we have every day is to look straight at what's going on right now and smile and have a good laugh on our-selves and say, "It's all good." Then add a huge thank you to God for making this life so magnificent that we can create *a brand new experience of it* in any given moment.

I have said that Observed Reality is a wonderful reality—it is a very high and rare state of experiencing, one which most people seldom reach. You would think that the Observed Reality would be the reality most often experienced by human beings, but it is, in fact, a very elevated state of consciousness that many people live their entire lifetime without entering more than occasionally. Most humans most of the time come from their Imagined Truth, and therefore experience a Distorted Reality.

You can tell if you are living in the Observed Reality because you will be clear that in this moment *there is nothing going on* other than *what is going on.*

The moment you bring your awareness to just what is happening now, you realize that everything "bad" that you think about this "now" is *stuff that you've added.* It's stuff that's not really there. You're *placing* it there, with your thought.

All you have to do to get rid of the pain of what is happening now is to stop *adding* the pain TO what is happening now. Pull the plug! Drain the moment of the bad past or the unwelcome future. Have a new thought about Right Now—and have it *right now!*

It's all good!

How can you say that when I just lost my job? you might growl—and that would be fair. Or, more sadly, *How can you say that when my loved one has just died? Or when my relationship has just ended?*

These are difficult, stress-filled moments. I am not suggesting they are not. Events such as these challenge every belief we may have that we live in a friendly universe. Only the soul's absolute knowing that, when all is said and done, everything is happening for the best of all concerned can bring us peace in a time such as this.

Life (and every condition and circumstance and relationship *in* life) is functional until its stability is threatened. In that case, it is adaptable. Thus, it renders itself sustainable by changing form.

This is what is occurring at the moment of a loved one's death—and at the moment of the death of anything . . . a relationship, a job, a way of life, anything at all. Nothing changes except for the better.

Right now you may be scoffing at this. Yet I'm going to go back to this: I'm willing to bet that if you assessed things very honestly you would agree that some of the worst things that ever happened to you were actually some of the best things that ever happened to you.

A Master sees this truth in *all* things. I am not a Master, nor anything close to it. Yet I can see that in my own life this has been true. You already know that fifteen years ago I had an automobile accident in which I broke my neck, which sent me into nearly two years of rehab, which required me to stop work, which caused me to lose my income, which eventually reduced me to living in a tent for an entire year, panhandling on street corners and struggling in all sorts of weather just to stay fed, warm, and dry.

Worst thing that could ever happen to a person, right? The great human nightmare, yes? Well . . . yes and no. At first, it was terrifying. I never imagined in my wildest dreams that I would become A Street Person. And once I was out there, living in that tent, I couldn't imagine how I was ever going to get back into a real house again.

Yet now, as I look back on it, I see that this was one of the greatest things that ever happened to me. It taught me lessons about life that I can't imagine I could have learned any other way. It brought me to a place of the greatest understanding of my own inner resources. It took me to a higher level of compassion and a deeper caring for every member of the human race. And it opened me to an awareness of God and the meaning of life that changed everything I thought I understood, carrying me to a new place of experiencing each moment as an unspeakable gift.

Okay, now you might say that this is a lucky case of "all's well that ends well," but I have learned that *everything* ends well if I let go and let God; if I simply allow whatever change is occurring in my life to occur without opposition.

This doesn't mean Do Nothing, but this does mean Do Not Resist.

What you resist persists. What you look at disappears. That is, it ceases to have its illusory form. Non-resistance delivers us from what is Imagined and awakens us to what is Apparent, finally showing us the Actual Truth. It is about ". . . delivering us from evil. . . ." Suddenly, options are open to us that seemed utterly blocked just moments before. Everything changes with a change in point of view.

That is the true power behind Change #7.

When you understand that all change happens in order to sustain harmony in the universe . . . when you *believe* that, even though it seems unbelievable . . . when you are certain that life was meant to be happy . . . and when you know that all stories can have wonderful endings if you do not block them with bitterness, anger, resentment, frustration, or non-belief in even the *possibility* of a wonderful ending (for most, the biggest block of all) . . . *then* you can change your thought about what is occurring—and thus, change your idea of what *will* occur.

Has your life not shown you that everything works out for your highest evolutionary purpose? Of course it has. The proof of this is that *you're still here*.

"Yes," you might say, "but look what I had to do to *get* here!" Agreed. It wasn't an easy road. Yet that is because you did not have the tools that you have now. And yet, even without these tools, you came through it all.

So . . . *what makes you think it will be any different tomorrow?*

We see, then, that the issue is not *whether* you're going to survive, but *how.* Will you be happy, or will you be sad? Will you be excited again about life, or will you be discouraged, disgruntled, and disappointed? Will you be a blessing to all whose lives you touch, or will you be a burden to everyone around you?

The way you hold the present experience is the way you create the next. And *that* is why changing your perspective about future change is so powerful.

The trick for you now is to transform this *insight* into *foresight.* The trick is to know this about your tomorrow, *today.* The trick is to be very clear that life is on your side.

This does not mean that everything always turns out the way you want it to. What it does mean is that sometimes what you want is not what is best for you.

What??? *Can that be true?* Is it possible to want something that is not even in one's own best interest? Of course it is. People do it all the time. That's because they do not always *recognize* what's in their own best interest. And *that* is because they do not know who they really are, where they are, what they are really doing here on this earth, and what the purpose of all of this is, anyway.

So answer those Four Fundamental Questions for yourself, then change your idea about future change. Drop the thought that you cannot affect the future. Tell yourself that the future is not coming TO you, it is coming THROUGH you.

The change that is coming to you in the future is that change that you *place* in your future with the thoughts, words, and actions of today. These are the three Tools of Creation, and if you would like more buttressing around this idea and an even deeper explanation of how you are the creator of your own reality, pick up a copy of *Conversations with God, Book 1* and give yourself the treat of one of the most inspirational and life-changing texts you will ever read.

If you have read it before, read it again. If you have never read it, do so now. Then see what you think. And take what resonates with you into your life as part of your own living truth.

Yes, yes, *yes* . . . change your idea about the changes to come, even as you change your idea about the changes that have passed. Then you can change your experience of both.

What is it that you were given?
I mean from the loss.
After, what was taken.
That very thing you could never
live without.
The person or place;
the secret, or circumstance—
now that it is gone,
or has been found out,
and you can no longer call it foundation,

what is it that you were given?

You know, and I know, this:
there is a hollowing out.
Something comes and opens you up

right
down
the
middle

and from that moment on
you are no longer immune to this world.

You wake, you wander,
every familiar, now a foreign.
You walk as through water

until you make it back to your bed
and finally, even there—
your sheets; your own pillow's scent different,
as if daily someone repaints your room, displaces something,
disturbs a cherished memento.

———————————

You see,
sometimes we are emptied.
We are emptied
because
Life wants us to know

so

much

more

Light.

—*'What Is It That You Were Given?'* © 2006 Em Claire

22.

THE EIGHTH CHANGE

Now look, we're getting to the end of our visit here and I want you to know that I understand the impact of what has happened to you in this time of change. Whether you've lost a job or lost a house or lost a relationship or lost your health or lost a loved one through death . . . whatever has changed, I understand how that has affected you. I am willing to join you in moving through that, as are the other spiritual life coaches who are reachable through www.ChangingChange.net.

Whether you use the support available to you in many forms there, or find assistance from other sources, I would advise you not to sidestep what you are going through right now. I would not want you to act as if it didn't happen, or pretend it doesn't matter that it did.

I want you to neither hide from it nor minimize it, but look at it squarely, and allow yourself whatever truth, emotion, and experience comes up for you around that—because I know that what you resist persists.

Then I invite you to add to your processing of all this by using some of the tools I have given you here. I invite you to look at the Apparent Truth and not just the Imagined Truth. I invite you to consider the possibility that your soul (and the soul of everyone else involved) knows exactly what it is doing, and that what it is doing is ultimately for the highest good of all concerned.

I want you, as well, to understand that the fact that this change has occurred does not mean that you cannot change this *change*—even possibly returning your life circumstance to something close to, and better than, what it was before (as in, for instance, a broken relationship that has been mended).

No possibility for the future is off the table.

I have spoken in my workshops to people who have lost millions, only to come back to make millions more. I have heard from people who lost their dearest relationship, only to come back to reconcile and raise it to heights never before imagined. I have talked to people who have been given a death sentence by their doctor, only to come back to a health so robust as to inspire the word "miracle."

Yes, I have heard from these people and more. Their stories are all different, yet there is one thing they all have in common. The end of their story *was not the end of their story.*

You've heard a lot from me about my own particular adventure, but let me just add this: I absolutely thought my story was over, that the good times were finished, more than once. My oh my oh my, how wrong I was. If I only knew then what I know now. Or, as my father used to say: *So old so soon, so smart so late.*

Let me help you get to where you want to be in life before you become an old person like me. Or, if you already are an old person like me, let me help you to ease your steps on the journey home.

My wonderful friends, I urge you to consider the possibility that life was meant to be happy.

Do you believe that? If you do not, then *run*, don't walk, to your nearest bookstore and pick up a copy of *Happier Than God.* This is one of the most exciting books I have ever been given the inspiration to produce, covering with incredible expansiveness the Process of Personal Creation (what some call the Law of Attraction) and exploring aspects that have been largely ignored in other examinations of this life principle. It will explain it all for you!

One of the ways that life demonstrates that it was meant to be happy is by giving us the tools with which to *recreate* our experience of life whenever we wish, in whatever way that we wish. If you haven't known what those tools are, *pay attention to what life is telling you right now.* Listen to what you have been hearing here.

And now, having heard all of that, it is time for you to make the Eighth Change. This has to do with the largest umbrella under which you now stand in this present stormy weather . . . your umbrella theory about life itself. I invite you now to make . . .

CHANGE #8:
Change your idea about life

Now it is time to consider the whole doggone process. Not just the process of *change*, not just the Mechanics of the Mind, not just the System of the Soul, but the entire episode that we are living from birth to death.

What is this here . . . what is going *on* . . . ? Yes, the mind has yearned for answers to these questions since the mind awakened you to your own existence. The problem is that most of our ideas have come from *before*. We take our collective ideas about *today* from what somebody else told us about *yesterday*—and from our own encounters with it.

But that makes sense, doesn't it? Oughtn't we be learning from our experience? *No!* Not if our experience has arisen out of an Imagined Truth rather than the Actual Truth. Not if our experience has led us to a Distorted Reality rather than the Ultimate Reality.

So if we are not to listen to our experience, then what *are* we to listen to . . . ?

Our soul. Our Being. Go back to the top of the clock. Go back to twelve o'clock high. We should be listening to the soul being, not the human being. And to the connection that our soul makes with the One Soul there is.

I believe that when you make that connection (meditate, pray, allow yourself contemplative moments, quietly read, quietly walk through the woods, quietly bathe and soak in the warm water of life, quietly write, quietly eat, quietly sing to yourself a song of the soul) . . . I believe that when you make that connection, you will hear from the still small voice within that life was not meant to be a struggle. Nor was it meant to be a "test." Nor was it meant to be a "baptism of fire" or a "trial" or a "school" or *anything at all unpleasant.*

I believe you will hear that, quite to the contrary, life was meant to be an overwhelming joy from first moment to last; a celebration of who you are and what you are capable of; an expression of glorious and wondrous proportion, the joyful explosion of Life itself into the arena of Life itself, *expanding Life itself through the process of Life itself.*

This is true locally, in your own life, and cosmically, in the life of the universe. On November 17, 2006, the Associated Press reported that the Hubble space telescope has shown that a mysterious form of energy first conceived by Albert Einstein appears to have been fueling the expansion of the universe for most of its history. Using supernova explosions to gauge the expansion of the universe, astronomers made a shocking observation.

> "It appeared that older supernovae, whose light had traveled a greater distance across space to reach the Hubble telescope, were receding from Earth more slowly than simple big-bang theory would predict. Nearby supernovae were receding more quickly than expected," the Associated Press story said, adding: "That could only be true if *some mysterious force* were causing the expansion of the universe to accelerate over time." (Italics mine.)

This "mysterious force" is Life itself. It is God, *Godding.* And it is operating inside your life—inside *you*—in every moment. When you are quiet with yourself you can feel this "mysterious force." Indeed, when you are quiet with yourself you quite literally *let the Force be with you.*

Now here is where things get interesting. This "force," or energy, *carries data.* Indeed, it is *the data itself.* Okay? Got that? *Energy is data. Data is energy.*

Have you ever heard anyone say that certain numbers contain "good energy"? It is true. The number nine, for instance, and equations that produce the number nine (8+1, 4+5, 3x3, etc.) are all said to be very powerful. I'm not a numerologist, but it wouldn't surprise me.

Acquiring, or accessing, the Data of Life is a matter of quieting the mind so that you can hear the soul, where that data is stored. Meditation is one way to do this. Everyone has heard of meditation, yet many people do not really know how to meditate. I've been asked many times in our spiritual renewal retreats if I could offer instruction in the best way to do this.

Of course, there is no "best way." My personal way of meditating is by writing. It is for me a very powerful meditation, and much of the time when I am supposedly writing I am actually staring off into space, not even thinking, but just *being* with what is moving through me in that moment, and opening—without question, expectation, or requirement—to what is coming next. (This is, of course, a wonderful way to journey through *all of life.*)

Although there is no one form of meditation that is "better" than another, so-called "sitting meditation" is what most people are most familiar with and want to know more about. So let me share with you some of my ideas around that.

Let's start by doing a little "quickie" meditation right here and now, just to give your mind a rest. For a brief moment, allow yourself to

Put the book down

Just close your eyes and breathe deeply, taking in three slow "sleeping" kind of breaths. Then just relax and continue being with yourself, quietly, for a while.

When you're ready, pick up the chapter at . . .

SOME IDEAS ABOUT MEDITATION

One thing I might suggest to people who have a difficult time quieting their mind is the practice of quiet, sitting meditation twice a day—fifteen minutes each morning and fifteen minutes each evening.

Try, if it is possible, to set a regular time when you will do this. Then see if you can stick to that time. Yet if you cannot keep such a consistent schedule, know that any time will do, so long as it is at least twice a day, early and late.

When you meditate you may want to sometimes sit outside, if it is nice and warm, allowing the morning sun to bake you, or the stars to sparkle above you. Inside, you might sit by a window and let the dawn sun pour in and the night sky enclose you. There is, as I said, no "right way" to do sitting meditation. (Indeed, there is no "right way" to do anything.)

One may sit in a comfortable chair, or on the floor, or upright in bed, for that matter. Choose what works for you.

Some people sit on the floor, usually with no back rest but occasionally against a wall or something, because floor sitting keeps them more "present" in the space. Some report to me that if they are too completely comfortable, as in an over-stuffed chair or on the bed, they tend to doze off or fade away from the moment; and if they are sitting on the floor, or out-side on the grass, that rarely occurs. They are totally mentally "present."

Once sitting, begin by paying attention to your breathing, closing your eyes, and simply listening to yourself inhaling and exhaling. Be in blackness and pay attention only to what you are hearing. When you have "united"—that's the only word I can find that fits here—with the rhythm of your breath, begin to expand your attention to what your "inner eye" is seeing.

Usually at that point this is nothing but darkness. If you are seeing images—that is, "thinking thoughts" of something and seeing those in your mind—work to fade those thoughts out, like a "fade to black" on the movie screen. Turn your mind to blankness. Focusing your inner eye, peer deeply into this dark-ness. Be looking for nothing in particular, but simply peering deeply, allowing yourself to search for nothing and need nothing.

In my own experience what happens next can often be the appearance of what appears to be a small, flickering blue "flame" or a burst of blue light piercing the darkness. I find that if I begin thinking about this cognitively—that is, defin-ing it, describing it to myself, trying to give it shape and form or make it "do" something or "mean" something—it disappears immediately. The only way that I can "make it come back" is to pay it no mind.

I have to work hard to turn my mind off and just be with the moment and the experience, without judging it, defining it, or trying to make something happen or figure it out or understand it from my logic center. It is rather like making love. Then, too, for the experience to be mystical and magical, I must turn my mind off and just be with the moment and the experience, without judging it, defining it, or trying to make something happen or figure it out or understand it from my logic center.

Meditation is making love to the universe. It is uniting with God. It is uniting with Self. It is not to be understood, created, or defined. One does not understand God, one simply experiences God. One does not create God, God simply is. One does not define God, God defines one. God IS the definer and the defined. God is the definition itself.

Insert the word Self wherever the word God appears in the above paragraph and the meaning remains the same.

Now, back to the dancing blue flame. Once you take your mind off it, all the while keeping your focus *on* it, without expectation or thought of any kind, the flickering light may reappear. The trick is to keep your mind (that is, your thought process) off it, all the while keeping your focus (that is, your undivided attention) on it.

Can you imagine this dichotomy? This means paying attention to what you are not paying attention to. It is very much like daydreaming. It is like when you are sitting in broad daylight, in the middle of some place of great activity, and you are paying attention to nothing at all—and to everything all at once. You are expecting nothing and requiring nothing and noticing nothing in particular, but you are so *focused* on the "nothing" and the "everything" that someone finally has to snap you out of it (perhaps by literally snapping their fingers), saying, "Hey! Are you *daydreaming*????"

Usually, one daydreams with one's eyes open.

Sitting meditation is "daydreaming with your eyes closed." That's as close as I can come to explaining the experience.

Now the dancing blue flame has reappeared. Simply experience it and do not try to define it, measure it, or explain it to yourself in any way. Just . . . fall into it. The flame will appear to come toward you. It will become larger in your inner field of vision. This is not the flame moving toward you at all, but *you* moving into, and inside of, the experience of *it*.

If you are lucky you will experience *total immersion* in this light before your mind starts telling you about it and talking to you about it, comparing it to Past Data. If you have even one instant of this mindless immersion, you will have experienced bliss.

This is the bliss of total knowing, total experiencing of the Self as One with everything, with the Only Thing There Is. You cannot "try" for this bliss. If you see the blue flame and begin to anticipate this bliss, the flame will disappear instantly, in my experience. Anticipation and/or expectation ends the experience. That is because the experience is happening in EverMoment, and anticipation or expectation *places it into the future, where you are not.*

Hence, the flame seems to "go away." It is not the light that has gone away, it is you. You have left EverMoment.

This has the same effect on your *inner* eye that closing your *outer* eyes has on your experience of the physical world around you. You quite literally shut it out. In my own experience this encounter with bliss comes but once every thousand moments of meditation. Having known it once is both a blessing and, in a sense, a curse, because I am forever wishing for it again. Still, there are times when I can retreat from the wishing, remove myself from the hope, desert my desires, reject my expectations, and place myself totally in the moment, utterly without anticipation of anything in particular. This is the mental state I seek to achieve. It is not easy, but it is possible. And if I achieve it, I have achieved mindlessness.

Mindlessness is not the emptying of the mind, but the focusing of the mind *away* from the mind. It is about being "out of our mind"—that is, away from your thoughts for a while (more on this later). This gets me very close to that place at the point between realms in the Kingdom of God, the space of Pure Being. This gets me very close to nirvana. This can carry me to bliss.

So . . . if you have managed to find a way to quiet your mind on a regular basis—through sitting meditation, what I call walking meditation, or "doing meditation" (doing the dishes can be a wonderful meditation, as can reading, or *writing,* a book), or stopping meditation (again, I'll get into this more later)—you have undertaken what may be the single most important commitment of your entire life: a commitment to your soul, to be *with* your soul, to *meet* your soul, to *hear* and *listen to* and *interact with* your soul.

In this way you will move through your life not only from the place of your mind, but your soul as well. This is what Ken

Wilbur, one of the most widely read and influential American philosophers of our time, refers to in his book *A Theory of Everything* as Integral Transformative Practice. The basic idea of an ITP, Wilbur says, is simple: "The more aspects of our being that we simultaneously exercise, the more likely that transformation will occur."

That's what we've been talking about here since our conversation began, of course. We've been talking about personal transformation—the altering of your individual experience of all of life, and particularly that basic, fundamental, essential part of life that we call *change*.

We've been talking about integrating all three parts of the Totality of Your Being in a cooperating, multifunctioning Whole. Yet one cannot do this unless and until one knows that one *is* a three-part being, and then understands thoroughly . . .

1. The Basics of the Body
2. The Mechanics of the Mind
3. The System of the Soul

We've not talked about the first of these three aspects of the triune expression of life that is you, and now is our time to do so. Are you ready to put the final piece of the puzzle into place? If your mind would like a little time to consider what we've just covered, you could always

Stop here for a while

It's as good a place as any to take a breath and take a break, to push back from the banquet table for just a moment. Then . . .

when you're ready, pick up the chapter at . . .

WHERE THE BODY COMES IN

"Your body is not something you are, it is something you have."

My friend Dr. Ilchi Lee, acknowledged before in this conversation for his brilliant thesis on the human brain, is fond of saying this. Other wonderful teachers and philosophers such as Jean Houston, Ken Wilbur, and Barbara Marx Hubbard make the same point.

More and more we are coming to understand that we are something *other than* the body, *other than* the mind, and yes, even *other than* the soul. We are *all three combined*, and the Whole is indeed greater than the sum of its parts.

The Whole Being that we are is pure energy—which might be called *Spirit.* Your body is an energy package. So, too, is your mind. Likewise, your soul. In short, you are a *spiritual being having a physical experience.*

Physicality should be understood to be illusory *in the sense that it is neither where you are nor who you are.*

Where you really are is in the place of Pure Being. This is also *who* you are. In the Kingdom of God, who you are, where you are, when you are, and what you are, are *all the same thing.*

You need to consider the implications of that statement for a while. You really do. I mean, we *all* do. It is our failure to consider those implications that creates the illusion in which we live—and the misery in which humanity is daily enmeshed.

I said that . . . who you are, where you are, when you are, and what you are, are *all the same thing*. I call this same thing "God." You can call it anything you wish, but you cannot ignore it, nor pretend that this larger context within which Life expresses itself does not exist.

We are talking here about your very Essence. This is the raw Energy of Life itself. That Energy, that Essence is not physical, but it *became* physical in order to Know Itself in its own Experience. For this is the triumvirate expression of Divinity:

The miracle of physicality is accomplished by The Energy and The Essence through a process that could best be described as "a quickening of the spirit."

The primal sound of the Universe is the lowest note in the score of God's symphony. It is the sound of *om* . . . a rumble so deep, it almost sounds ominous. In recent years, deep-space listening devices have actually been able to pick up this sound. It is the Original Vibration. It is The Energy and The Essence, oscillating at its slowest speed.

When this speed increases, the pitch goes up, from a deep rumble to the gentle melody of life as we know it. Everything begins with the First Vibration. Everything begins with sound ("In the beginning was the Word. . . ."). And The Sound said, *Let there be Light.* And it oscillated Itself so fast that its very Essence became *white hot.* And Light was born.

And then, through the simple yet elegant process of shifting its oscillation between various frequencies, The Energy and The Essence produced other manifestations of physicality. And the deep sound of *om* became the sweet sight of life. ("And the Word was made flesh, and dwelt among us.")

The faster The Energy and The Essence vibrated—that is, the higher the *frequency* of its oscillations—the more solid that which is *not* solid appeared.

Think of it this way: if a point of energy can move rapidly enough in a straight line between Point A and Point B, it will appear to be at neither Point A *nor* Point B, but at every point in between. Its incomprehensible speed makes it appear to the human eye to be nowhere in particular at any given moment, but *everywhere at once*—because it is moving so fast, we can't "spot" it in any single block of time and space. Therefore, the rapidity of its movement makes it appear as *a solid line* between A and B.

You can prove this to yourself with a little experiment. Paste a big black dot on the end of a transparent straw. Now hold the straw in front of your face and move it left-to-right against the background of a white wall. You will see the dot move, of course, and you will be able to point out exactly where it is at any moment. Now, increase the speed with which you move the dot, finally getting to the place where you are moving your hand back and forth so fast that the dot cannot be seen as being in one place or the other, but, in fact, in all places at once. If you squint just a bit this will appear to the naked eye to be a straight line.

The human mind cannot compute the data that it is seeing fast enough to keep up with the *new* data it is seeing. The data stream is faster than the mind's ability to analyze it. Therefore, the mind does not know what it is seeing.

The world is 2 percent matter and 98 percent space, but it looks to us "for all the world" as if it is *exactly the other way around.*

Thus, we live in a world of our illusion. Yet it was purposefully created this way by the Originating Intelligence. The mind is a device beautifully designed to analyze a limited amount of data from an unlimited source. It was *never intended* to comprehend *all of it at once.* That is the job of the soul.

Likewise, the body is a device.

Your body is the physicalization of Spirit in a particular form in a particular place at a particular time for a particular purpose having to do with the Particularization of Every Particle of The All.

The All is that which is *not particular*. It is Everything—and therefore, it is nothing *in particular*. Yet The Everything could not experience Itself as Everything, since there was Nothing Else with which to compare it. So, It chose to *individuate* Itself in order that All That Is could experience Itself as *something in particular*.

This Process of Particularization created what I have here called the Realm of the Physical. Again, it is a process by which the primal vibration simply increased the frequency of its oscillation.

The All of you is wonderful—that is, full of wonder—yet your body is the least of these. Next comes your mind, and the most wonderful of all is your soul. Your mind is so wonder-full that it can actually impact your body . . . and, indeed, all things physical.

That is, your mind can create your physical reality. I said . . . *your mind can create your physical reality.*

Not only *can it* do this, it *is* doing this. Your mind is creating your reality every minute of every day, whether you know it or not. The question is not whether the You that you are is creating your reality, the question is only whether you are doing it consciously or unconsciously.

You make things physical in your reality through *a quickening of the Spirit.* This is the benefit of what you might call *fast thinking.* You know how people are praised for being a fast thinker? There is more to that appellation than you might have imagined.

You would be amazed at how fast your mind can think. It can think twice as fast as it ordinarily thinks through the simple process of *ignoring all Past Data.* You might call this

Skipping Past the Past. And the extraordinary insight is that you can instruct your mind to do this; you can *train your mind to do this.*

How? How can you train your mind to ignore everything it thinks it knows about a subject? By making a quantum leap to the awareness of the soul.

Always, in every moment, the decision you get to make is, shall I consider the data of the mind or the awareness of the soul? When you move to the awareness of the soul you raise your consciousness to the top of the triangle, to the place of Being.

To be or not to be, that is the question.

Now here is the irony of how everything I've just described works . . . are you ready for the supreme irony? This is a secret of secrets; that which no one has ever told you:

In order to access the awareness of the soul, you need to *slow down.*

Now wait a minute! Didn't I just say that you had to "think fast"? Yes! You have to *think fast* when things are happening around you . . . fast enough to tell yourself to *slow down.*

The first thing your mind will want to do when incoming data is deluging you is *analyze the data* and present you with *all your options for response.* It does this very, very rapidly. In order for you to short-circuit this process you must "think fast." *So* fast that as your mind begins to take you deep into your Past Data about what is going on right now, you literally *stop your mind from going there.* You Skip Past Your Past.

Then you re-route your energy (your mind, you know, *is* electrical energy! You can physically measure the impulses). You route your energy to Awareness rather than Data. This is like switching tracks in a train yard, from the track that just goes back around to where the train has just *been*, to a spur that takes it to a place of rest. You can do this quite literally on the *spur of the moment*, moving from the mind to the soul. You know how some people are described as having a "one-track mind"? This is about changing that. There are times when we all have a one-track mind. We keep thinking about what we're thinking about—going to all the same places over and over. As you would know if you rode an actual train through its entire route, *this gets you nowhere.* You wind up right back where you started.

Soooo . . . to change all that, *you have to be fast enough to slow down.*

You have to be quick enough to stop your mind from racing on, and slow your process of particularization, dropping your vibe to the level of your soul-frequency. Your soul's oscillation is so slow that *you cannot see it.*

Now I know that this is the exact reverse of everything you've ever learned, everything you've ever been told. You've been told to "raise your vibration," and that enlightenment is about "consciousness-raising." Actually, it's just the opposite. It's about lowering your vibration. It's about slowing down to the frequency rate of the Invisible. It's about getting closer to the Primal Sound. That is why monks and some others who meditate often sit together and chant the sound of *Om* in a deep, rich tone. It is about slowing down the vibe. It is about being out of your mind.

The place of your body in all of this? It is, as I said, simply and only an instrument. The question is, are you using it as an instrument of the mind or an instrument of the soul? And what I am saying here is that, at best, it should be *an instrument of both.*

I don't want to paint the mind as the enemy here. It is not. Most decidedly, it is a miracle machine. Yet we must let the mind do what the mind was designed to do, and the soul do what the soul was created to do. We must remember that we are tri-part beings, and that the body—also a "miracle machine"—is nevertheless the least of the three. It is a *device*, there to do our bidding.

Do not, therefore, get caught up in things of the body. Take care of the body, for sure—just as you would take care of your car or your home or any other valuable possession. Yet do not confuse yourself about Who You Are.

You are not the body. You are not the mind. You are not even the soul. You are all three—and more. You are the Spirit that *forms* all three. You are The Energy. You are The Essence.

Please do not regret
all those moments that have brought you
Here.
If you are reading this,
then your perseverance has been answered,
and a Grace is coming.
So for now, hold on loosely to where you are.
And like knots on a rope that mark your reaching,
hand over hand
you will continue to climb—
sometimes through ecstasy,
sometimes through white agony,
higher
into evermore light.
This same formula over
and over again.
Until that day you find yourself
just a beacon;
only flame.
In a place
where even *Love Itself* has come undone.

—'*Love Itself*' © 2006 Em Claire

23.

LIFE'S WONDER

I HAVE KNOWN MANY people who never really think about life. "I'm too busy," they tell me. "I'll leave that to writers and poets."

For this reason many people find themselves living in a world where stuff is going on that no one seems to want to have going on. How it is possible for six billion people to want the same thing and not be able to get it? they ask. What kind of a world *is* this? they want to know. Or, in the words of that heart-sinking song by Peggy Lee from so many years ago, "Is that all there is?" If that's all there is . . . somebody *send in the clowns,* because this has got to be a circus.

But it's not a circus, it's a beautifully orchestrated symphony, with God as the conductor and all of us as the musicians. All we have to do to make beautiful music together is know the score.

When we see life as it really is, it all suddenly makes sense. Then the changes that are occurring are seen as gifts and not burdens. And then future changes will be demonstrations of creation, not tests of endurance.

Life is a process. It is not something that is "just happening," it is something that is happening *on purpose*. There is something that life is designed to do. *What is the outcome that life is trying to produce?*

That is the question of the hour. Indeed, of the *century.* The answer can be offered at two levels . . .

UNIVERSALLY: Life is the process by which God *expresses* God, *experiences* God, and *expands* God.

INDIVIDUALLY: Life is intended to produce for you a direct experience of who you really are—and then, an opportunity to go to the next level in your expression of that.

Put simply, the purpose of life is to know life and to express more life through the process of life itself, manifested through all the individuations of life—in this *particular* case: You.

Life meets its purpose through the process called Change.

That is, Life (God) is always changing in order to always be creating and recreating Itself anew, in a way that expands Itself.

Many people in the world think that God (as opposed to humans) causes Change, in the sense that God causes everything. Ah, but does God? Is there even a God at all (in the sense of a Supreme Being existing apart and separate from us) who would or could do that? And if there is, why would God cause one Change and not another? Why would God do "this" and not "that," favor this person or project and not that one? What are God's *criteria?*

Yes, there are those who believe that God is pulling the levers, for reasons known only to Him and, presumably, those who follow the One True Religion (whatever religion that might be in any particular case).

So what is true about all this? *Is* "God" pulling the levers? Or is life a process that runs all by itself?

The answer is no to both questions. "God" (as that separate, Supreme Being) is not pulling the levers . . . *and* . . . life is not a process that runs all by itself.

Life's wonder is that it is a process in which *you*, as a sentient being filled with the consciousness of self-awareness, have the opportunity to create your own experience and your own reality, to know yourself as you appear to be, to express yourself as you came to be, and finally, to recreate yourself as you wish to be in the next grandest version of yourself. Life's wonder is that the whole human race, *jointly*, has the same opportunity! We are, daily, co-creating our collective reality.

Life's wonder is that it is a glorious adventure and a sweet, sweet journey, and I know and understand that it does not appear to be that way for many, many people. Indeed, it is when I see the suffering of others that I am the most tempted to give up my idea about life's wonder, about this being a friendly universe, and about God being a friendly God.

We talked about this earlier, and I have been given answers to this riddle often. Yet there are still times when my mind is perplexed and my heart is heavy and only my soul is at peace in the midst of all of the travail that I witness being visited upon the lives of others, if not in my own life.

Why the travail? I ask, even though I have been given the answer. *Why the tragedies?* I cry.

And the One Soul replies . . .

> Once again, my sweet, caring, compassionate one, you do not and cannot know of the "soul assignment" which has been given to—and accepted by—another blessed Individuation of God. Yet can you not believe Me when I tell you that no Aspect of Divinity can be, at the soul level, victimized or damaged in any way? I know that at the human level, hurt and victimization exist. Yet I tell you this: outward manifestation is part of the inward journey of all entities and cannot be fully explained or understood in human terms because of the limitations of the current human perspective. Yet this perspective can shift. And it will. All the human race needs is one more Shifter here and there, one more person committed to the Change that will Change Everything.

The One Soul then inspired me to write this:

> Let me see if I can give you a speck of an insight into a much higher and far more complex truth than what you may have previously considered. Have you ever done something for yourself or for another or for a cause that looked like it hurt or damaged you in some way—but you did it anyway, for the larger good?

I thought about that for a while. I remembered things I have done for myself that "looked like" they hurt or damaged me, but that really, in the long run, were "for my own good." I immediately came up with a good-sized list.

Then I took a look at things I have done for others that did me no good at all—that, in fact, actually damaged me in some way—but that I did anyway, because I loved that other person, or that project. Again, I came up with a pretty healthy list.

Now the One Soul inspired me to ask myself:

> Can you begin to understand how souls could be doing the same kind of thing? Does it seem to you possible that soul-beings would do this as part of their journey—to advance either their own evolution . . . or the evolution of another?

I had to admit that suddenly I had a better conceptual understanding of all of this. Then I suddenly saw a "movie" in my head. I was caused to imagine an exchange between myself and another soul. In my vision I was walking down a sidewalk in some city and I came across a street person leaning up against a building, clothes a mess, hair oily from not having been washed in weeks, and smelling . . . well, *interesting* . . . for lack of a better description.

The street person held out a small paper cup as I passed by. "Would you have any spare change?" she mumbled.

Oh, this same person is on this same spot six days out of seven, I said to myself. She's got a real racket going. Why bother even looking for work when you can pick up who knows how many dollars a week just standing here asking for it?

I passed her by without giving her so much as a look . . . but then I turned back and headed straight for her. "Tell me something," I blurted. "Why don't you just get a job like everybody else rather than standing here asking people for money?"

"If I did," the bag lady replied, "who would be here to let you see who you really are—?"

I was stunned by her answer.

Stunned into silence.

I invite you, now, to move into that silence yourself. Consider her reply. How does it feel to you? What is your intuitive response? Please give this some thought as you prepare to move into the final chapter of this book; as you prepare to embrace The Final Change . . .

"Show yourself to me,"
said I to God again.

And this is what happened next:

I became pregnant with Light.
My eyes were sunrise and sunset, both.
Freckles announced themselves planets and stars,
and beamed upon my cheeks.
Each of my lips became a kiss to the other,
my ears heard oceans of life.
Between my eyes there was an indigo wheel,
between my toes, blond fields.
My hands remembered climbing-trees,
my hair, each Lover's fingers.

And then I whispered,
"But why have you made me this way?"
And it was told to me:

"Because I have never had Your name before,
nor heard the way You sing it.
Nor stared into the Universe through eyes like These.
Nor laughed This way, nor felt the path that These tears take.

Because I have not known These ecstasies
nor risen to These heights, nor experienced
every nuance of the Innocence
with which you create your lows,

nor how a Heart could grow so wide,
or break so easily
or Love

quite so unreasonably."

—*'Unreasonably'* © 2008 Em Claire

24.

THE NINTH CHANGE

HERE IS WHAT I now understand: Some souls co-create experiences that are clearly (on a human level) hurtful and damaging to themselves. Nobody can know why they are doing this.

Maybe they have come to their present incarnation in order to experience the "other end" of something they have done to others in a previous lifetime.

Maybe they have come to allow other souls a chance to experience themselves in a particular way.

Maybe they have come to provide "players" or "actors" for some larger "scene" in the whole drama of life, the acting out of which will permit huge numbers of humans to come to a singular realization at once. (Those who were killed in the 9/11 tragedies come to mind . . . as do the millions murdered in the Holocaust.)

I cannot know, and I cannot pretend to know, the soul-agenda of the people who die of starvation or are sexually abused or have suffered one loss after the other in their lives or who in some other way have lived lives of struggle, pain, and sadness.

I can only keen for them, yearn for them to have their suffering end, notice the part of me that wants *no one* to suffer and *nothing* to be abused, and, as Mary O'Malley advises, let my heart break as I do—because as my heart breaks, my heart *opens*. I can only stand in honor of them and of their sacrifice and of their journey and of the soul choices they have made in order to *take* their journey.

Then I can decide who *I am* in relationship to them.

Who am I, and who do I choose to be, in relationship to the starving children of the world? Who am I, and who do I choose to be, in relationship to the oppressed and the downtrodden? Who am I, and who do I choose to be, in relationship to the disaffected and the disadvantaged, the disavowed and the disconnected, the dispossessed and the disenfranchised? Who am I and who do I choose to be?

That is the question. *That* is what life gives me an opportunity to decide. And likewise, who am I and who do I choose to be in relationship to my own incredibly good fortune, the gifts I have been given, the talents I have been allowed to nurture, the kindnesses I have been granted, the opportunities I have been offered, the intelligence I have been permitted to possess, the success I have been able to experience?

What do I want to make of this life, and of my Sacred Self in relationship *to* it? *That* is the question. *That* is what life gives me an opportunity to decide. And my life *lived* is my decision and my answer.

You are faced with the same opportunity. And this much I know. The universe is conspiring in your favor. It is placing before you in every moment all of the right and perfect people, circumstances, and situations with which to answer life's only question: Who am I.

Have you decided yet?

As I'm sure you know, there are two ways to decide anything. One way is to decide it, and the other way is to not decide it. Yet always remember: *Not to decide is to decide.*

The important thing is not to allow yourself to be defined by default. If you think you are making no decision by making no decision, you are making a mistake. If you are not careful, the biggest decision you will ever make could be the decision you never made.

So let's be clear: all of life is a deciding. You are deciding . . . with every truth you embrace, with every thought you birth, with every emotion you express, with every experience you produce . . . you are deciding Who You Are and Who You Choose to Be.

Every act is an act of self-definition.

All the changes in the collective experience of humanity have been created through the collective experience of humanity—and all the changes in the singular experience of your life have been created though the singular experience of your life. I said it before and I'll say it again: Life is an energy that feeds off the energy of Life Itself. Life is self-nourishing and self-creative. Life informs life about life through the process of life itself.

When a change occurs in your life it is because something in your life was not working, *and you sought to change that.* You may not think that you did—you may not have any conscious awareness that you did—but you did, I promise you. You and those who co-created with you.

Let me give you just one example of how this can occur.

A man comes home from work every day in a sour mood about life at the office. He has come to dislike his job, despise his boss, disrespect his co-workers, and disparage the whole company. He is a clever man, though, and since he does not yet have even the slightest prospect of another job, he manages to cover his true feelings very well. He says nothing untoward, offers no criticism, displays no antipathy, and is seen on the surface as nothing but a loyal, model employee.

After months of this he is suddenly laid off. Downsized. Let go. He can't figure it out. *What did he do to deserve this?* Nothing. The answer is, nothing. But he did do something to *create* it. His negative energies, inward and hidden as they were, created the energy field from which emerged the outcome with which he is abruptly faced.

Do you believe this? Do you believe that this is the way something like this can happen? Trust me. *This is exactly the way it happens.*

"As a man thinketh in his heart, so is he." If he thinks day and night, "I hate this place—I wish I didn't have to be here anymore," his wish will come true—even if he never utters a word about it. Life is like a genie let out of the bottle: It says: *Your wish is my command.*

Now let's take your own current situation. Unlike the man in the above little story who hated his work, what's going on in your life right now is a change that you did not wish (in even in your most private thoughts) would happen. This all came down against your *will.* So how does *that* work?

Simple. You may not have wished that this change would take place, but at some level you must have known that it could, and even might. And this was not a small knowing. It was a big knowing, in your heart.

It is your knowing that creates the strongest energy, not your wishing. In fact, *knowing* trumps *wishing* every time. That's because knowing has enormous power behind it. Wishing is wimpy, flimsy. "Knowing of a certainty" is the kind of faith that moves mountains. Someone once said, "What you know is what is so."

You can wish to win the million-dollar lottery, but if you *know* that you don't stand much of a chance, then you won't stand much of a chance. You can wish to get a date with the most desirable person in the class, but if you *know* that you don't stand much of a chance, then you won't stand much of a chance. You can wish to feel just fine about the huge change that is happening in your life, but if you *know* that you don't stand much of a chance, then you won't stand much of a chance.

Ah, yes . . . "if only wishing could make it so. . . ."

Well, wishing is a good start. Jiminy Cricket was right about that. But in the end, you must turn that wish into an awareness that your wish will come true. You must *know* that it will.

But what do you tell yourself *then* if, after all is said and done, it just doesn't happen? You must let yourself remember that you are always creating at three levels of creation: the subconscious level, the conscious level, and the super-conscious level. It is at the super-conscious level that you join with all other souls in a collaboration of cosmic proportion that allows for the perfect conditions to exist, allowing the souls involved to evolve to the next highest level.

So the reality that you have produced, the change that you are experiencing this minute, is not something that you created alone. The fact is that you created it in collaboration with others. All the other "players" in your Game of Life created it with you. You created the outcome together. For reasons known very clearly by the lot of you. In a way that serves the agenda of all of you.

This is just one more way of saying that everything happens for the best.

Now when you *know* that everything happens for the best, then everything that happens is okay with you. The irony of this is that *when everything that happens is okay with you, you set up an energy field of such equanimity and harmony with the universe that the universal law of attraction draws more equanimity and harmony into your life.*

Your soul knows that the process of co-creation never impinges upon the individual will of anyone. Nothing can happen against your inner will. Not even your death. *Especially* not your death. (For a thorough and inspiring exploration of this particular insight, see *Home with God in a Life That Never Ends.*)

Given Who and What you are (Divinity Individuated), it is impossible for anything to take place that violates your highest desire. The interweavings of life are always in harmony with each other. You must, therefore, have at some level agreed with all that has occurred and is occurring. If it happened *to* you, it happened *through* you.

This is why the soul is never unhappy. Why would the soul be unhappy when it is always getting what it wants?

Why it would *want* what it is getting is another question. The answer: there is always a reason tied to the soul's desire to evolve. Sometimes the soul evolves most rapidly by giving *up* what the mind wants, in favor of what someone else may need, or what a situation may require. The mind might not always be okay with this, but the soul always is.

So do not recriminate against yourself. Do not make yourself wrong or chastise or castigate yourself for any life outcomes that you have generated, consciously or unconsciously, that you would call negative. Rather, have compassion with yourself if you do not understand the larger reason for these outcomes, then give praise to yourself for your ability to meet them head on, then congratulate the magnificent part of yourself that finds a way to move through them, and finally, celebrate that aspect of yourself that sees, in the final analysis, the *benefit* that has come to you as a result of them.

You will know that you have changed your idea about life when you come to the last conclusion first. You will see life and everything *in* life as an opportunity, not an obstruction; as good fortune, not misfortune; as a gift, not a gaff. And your attitude about life itself will *recreate* itself in life itself.

After you've changed your idea about life and its purpose, you are only one step away from changing your idea about yourself—from changing your very identity.

Do this, and you will change everything. And *that* is something you may wish to

Take time to ponder

Only when you're ready, pick up the chapter at . . .

WALKING HOME

William Shakespeare had it exactly right:
There are more things in Heaven and Earth, Horatio, than are dreamt of in your philosophy.

The final change in our list of nine could very well be the first. If the entire human race ever made a wholesale shift to this new way of thinking, to this new way of holding the life experience itself, then every moment in every day in the life of every person in the world would be transformed forever. I now invite you to make this final change. I now invite you to . . .

CHANGE #9:
Change your identity

When I was a child—indeed, from the time I was eight or nine until the time I left my family of origin—my father repeatedly asked me the same question, usually about once every other week or so:
Who do you think you are anyway . . . ?

His question was borne of frustration, but if he thought *he* was frustrated, he should have lived in *my* reality! I had no idea who I was or what I was doing here, nor did I have any concept at all about what life was, or why it was the *way* it was. I couldn't understand it, I didn't agree with it, and I wanted no part of it. Yet getting out of it was not an attractive option.

(Actually, there were times when I actually thought that it might be. I am so happy to say that I moved through those times without succumbing to the temptation to end the most magnificent experience a soul could ever have. My process was a little herky-jerky, for sure. A little bumpy, no question. But I made it. Thank you, God!)

I came to the hope that somewhere, *somewhere*, there was an answer to all of this; a reason for it all; a way that it all made some sense. I figured that there was just something that I didn't understand, the understanding of which would change everything.

After my conversations with God I knew that I would never find what that "something" was in the Past Data held by the mind. I knew that I would have to somehow connect with a larger source. I knew that I was going to have to commune on a regular basis with my soul.

This I did in my own way. I've already said that there is more than one way to meditate. The meditation technique I described earlier is one way—and one very good way—to go about silencing the mind and connecting with the soul. But it is not the only way, nor is it necessarily, for everyone, the best way.

There are many people who find it extremely difficult to sit in silent meditation. For them, it may seem as if the "art of meditation" is something that is lost to them. I felt this way for a long time, because I am an impatient person by nature and sitting in silent meditation was not a thing I tolerated well. Then someone introduced me to Walking Meditation, and everything changed for me around the idea of "meditation." Suddenly, it was something I could *do.*

The first thing that happened when I learned about Walking Meditation is that my whole idea about what meditation *is* completely vanished, to be replaced by a much more clear and concise picture of what was going on. For me, meditation always meant "clearing the mind of everything," leaving the space for "the emptiness" to appear, so that I could move in consciousness into "the nothingness that is The All . . . ," or something like that.

What I was supposed to be trying to do, I thought, was "empty my mind." I was supposed to try to sit in one place, close my eyes, and "think of nothing." This made me crazy, because my mind never turns off! It is always thinking, thinking, *thinking* of *something.* So I was never very good at sitting with my legs crossed, closing my eyes, and concentrating on The Nothing. Frustrated, I hardly ever meditated—and envied those who said they did (although I secretly wondered whether they really did, or simply went through the motions, doing no better than I was able to do).

Then a master teacher in my life told me that I had entirely the wrong idea of what meditation was about. Meditation, she said, was not about *emptiness*, it was about *focus.* Instead of trying to sit still and think about nothing, she suggested that I do a "walking meditation" and move about, stopping to *focus* on specific things that my eyes would light upon.

"Consider a blade of grass," she would say. "Consider it. Look at it closely. Regard it intently. Consider every aspect of it. What does it look like? What are its specific characteristics? What does it feel like? What is its fragrance? What is its size, compared to you? Look at it closely. What does it tell you about Life?"

Then, she said, *"Experience the grass in its Completeness.* Take off your shoes and socks and walk on the grass in your bare feet. Think of nothing else but your feet. Focus your attention on the bottom of your feet and consider immensely exactly what you are feeling there. Tell your mind to feel nothing else, just for that moment. Ignore all other incoming data except the data coming from the bottom of your feet. Close your eyes, if this helps.

"Walk slowly and deliberately, allowing each slow and gentle step to tell you about the grass. Then open your eyes and look at all of the grass around you. Ignore all other incoming data except the data about the grass, coming from your eyes and feet.

"Now focus on your sense of smell, and see if you can smell the grass. Ignore all other incoming data except the data about the grass coming from your nose, your eyes, and your feet. See if you can focus your attention in this way. If you can, you will experience the grass as you may never have experienced it before. You will *know* more about grass than you ever knew before, at a deeper level. You will never experience it in the same way again. You will realize that you have been *ignoring the grass* your whole life."

Then, my master teacher said, do the same thing with a flower. "Consider it. Look at it closely. Regard it intently (that is, with *intention*). Consider every aspect of it. What does it look like? What are its specific characteristics? What does it feel like? What is its fragrance? What is its size, compared to you? Look at it closely. What does it tell you about Life?"

Then, she said, *"Experience the flower in its Completeness.* Bring it to your nose and smell it once more. Think of nothing else but your nose. Focus your attention on your nose and consider immensely exactly what you are experiencing there. Tell your mind to experience nothing else, just for that moment. Ignore all other incoming data except the data coming from your nose. Close your eyes, if this helps.

"Now focus on your sense of touch, and touch the flower carefully. Touch the flower at the same time as you smell the flower. Ignore all other incoming data except the data about the flower coming from your fingertips and your nose. Now, open your eyes and look closely at the flower. See if you can still smell the flower, now that it is far enough away for you to look at it and touch it. See if you can focus your attention in this way. If you can, you will experience the flower as you may never have experienced it before. You will *know* more about the flower than you ever knew before, at a deeper level. You will never experience it in the same way again. You will realize that you have been *ignoring the flowers* your whole life."

Then, she said, do the same thing with a tree. Walk over to a tree and consider it. "Look at it closely. Regard it intently. Consider every aspect of it. What does it look like? What are its specific characteristics? What does it feel like? What is its fragrance? What is its size, compared to you? Look at it closely. What does it tell you about Life?"

And she said, *"Experience the tree in its Completeness.* Place you hands upon it and feel it totally. Think of nothing else but your hands. Focus your attention on your hands and consider immensely exactly what you are experiencing there. Tell your mind to experience nothing else, just for that moment. Ignore all other incoming data except the data coming from your hands. Close your eyes, if this helps.

"Now focus on your sense of smell, and smell the tree. Continue touching the tree at the same time as you smell the tree. Ignore all other incoming data except the data about the tree coming from your fingertips and your nose. Now, open your eyes and look closely at the tree. Look up at it, and see if you can climb in consciousness to its top. See if you can still smell the tree, now that it is far enough away for you to look at it. Keep touching it. See if you can focus your attention in this way. If you can, you will experience the tree as you may never have experienced it before. You will *know* more about the tree than you ever knew before, at a deeper level. You will never experience it in the same way again. You will realize that you have been *ignoring the trees* your whole life."

"Now, step away from the tree and lose all physical contact with it. See if you can bring to your mind the experience of the tree as you stand and look at it from farther away. Experience it completely. Do not be surprised if you can smell the tree, even from a distance. Do not be surprised if you can, in a sense, even 'feel' the tree from where you are. What has happened is that you have *opened yourself* to the vibration of the tree. You are 'catching the vibe.' See how far back you can step from the tree and still retain 'contact.' When you lose touch with the experience of the tree, move closer in, move back to it. See if this helps you regain contact.

"These exercises," she said, "will help you develop your ability to *focus your attention* on whatever you want to *experience at a heightened level.*"

"Now, walk. Walk wherever you live. In the country, in the city, it does not matter. Walk slowly, but deliberately. And look around you. Let your eyes fall where they may. As your eyes find something, focus the fullness of your attention upon it. It can be anything. A garbage truck. A stop sign. A crack in the sidewalk, a pebble by the road. Look at it closely, from right where you are. Regard it intently. Consider every aspect of it. What does it look like? What are its specific characteristics? What does it feel like, from where you are? What is its fragrance? Can you sense that from where you are? What is its size, compared to you? Look at it closely. What does it tell you about Life?"

"Continue your walk. Pick out three things on your walk to consider in this way. This walk should take you at least a half hour. You cannot consider three things fully in less time, at first. Later, you will be able to consider something fully in just a moment, in a nanosecond. But now, you are just practicing.

"This is Walking Meditation, and what you are doing is training your mind to *stop ignoring* everything you are experiencing. You are training your mind to *focus* on a particular aspect of your experience, so that you may experience it completely."

Practice Walking Meditation in this way for three weeks, my master teacher told me, and "you will never experience life the same way again." Then, take the final step in Walking Meditation. Walk outside—or inside, for that matter. You can actually walk anywhere. From the bedroom to the kitchen will do. There is plenty to see, plenty to touch, plenty to experience. You can spend three hours with the carpet alone—and this time, she said, "do not pick out any particular part of what you are seeing or encountering. Try to encounter *all of it.* Seek to embrace *all of it.* Attempt to focus on *all of it at the same time.*

"Take in the Big Picture. Close your eyes at first, if this helps. Smell what you are smelling, hear what you are hearing, feel whatever you are 'feeling' of the space around you. Then open your eyes and add sight. See everything you are seeing, and nothing in particular. See All Of It. Smell All Of It. Feel All Of It. If this begins to overwhelm you, refocus on a Part Of It, so that you do not lose your psychic balance.

"With enough practice, you will soon be able to walk into any space or place and begin to experience All Of It at some level. You will realize then that you have been literally *walking home.* You have heightened your Awareness. You have raised your consciousness. You have expanded your ability to be Present, fully, in the moment.

"Now, do this with your eyes closed and while you are sitting down, and you have Silent Meditation. Boom. It is as simple as that."

With that my master teacher smiled at me. "Then try this with sex," she said. "Once you experience sex in this way, you will never want to experience it any other way again. You will realize that, all your life, *you have been ignoring what is really going on.*"

And she laughed.

Next I will tell you about Stopping Meditation. For now, just walk well. I never thought it was polite to say this, but it *is!* I am going to tell you now to

Take a walk

And only when you're ready, continue at . . .

STOPPING MEDITATION

There are many ways to meditate, and it was a wonderful discovery when I learned this. One of the most powerful forms of meditation for me is what I have called Stopping Meditation. The reason this is so powerful for me is that it can be done anywhere, and it takes very little time. Therefore, it is perfect for busy people "on the go."

Stopping Meditation means just that. It means we stop whatever we are doing for just a moment and pay attention to something about it. We dissect it in that moment and then look closely at one of its individual pieces.

This is a little bit different from Walking Meditation in that it does not take a half hour or more, as Walking Meditation can take. In Walking Meditation we deliberately take a walk for the deliberate purpose of deliberately focusing on a deliberate experience. In Stopping Meditation we do not use nearly as much time, but we can accomplish the same thing: *focus.*

Stopping Meditation can be used in the midst of a very busy day. *Combined* with Sitting Meditation and Walking Meditation it can create a powerful Trio of Tools that can dramatically alter your reality and raise your consciousness within a very short period of time. Yet even if used as the only form of meditation, it can be transformative.

Here is how Stopping Meditation works: decide that six times today (and every day) you will stop whatever you are doing for ten seconds and look closely and intently at one of its component pieces.

Let's say you are washing the dishes. Stop what you are doing for ten seconds—just *stop* in the middle of it—and peer deeply inside one aspect of what you are doing. Look, perhaps, at the water. See it splashing on the dishes. See if you can count the drops of water on the dish in your hand. Just count the water drops. I know it is an impossible task, but undertake to do it anyway, just for ten seconds.

Consider the wonder of the water. Look deeply into it. Peer inside. *Go* inside, in your consciousness. See what you experience there, see what you find. Just stop for a tiny moment and appreciate that moment in a singular way.

Okay, now the ten seconds are up. Now pull yourself out of that highly focused reality and back into the larger space of your experience. Don't get "lost" in it. Blink your eyes rapidly, or snap your finger, and literally snap out of it. Then, notice what you experienced for that brief moment.

Now go on with what you were doing. Yet don't be surprised if it takes on a whole new quality.

What you have done is truly appreciate something. To "appreciate" something is to make it larger, to increase it—as property, for instance, appreciates in value. When you use Stopping Meditation, you increase the value of your life. And of life itself. It has been my experience that this inevitably returns me to a place of peace.

In order to remind yourself to do this six times a day you may wish to have a little timer with you, or set your watch to beep. Later, as you get used to doing this, your stopping will come automatically to you. You will do this without having to be reminded.

Walking down the street, you will simply stop for a moment and select a portion of what you are seeing and see it again, in a deeper way. You will know what you already know about that, but you will know it in a deeper way. This is called "knowing again," or re-cognizing. The purpose of all of your life is simply this: to know again, to recognize, what is true, and Who You Really Are.

There are a thousand ways to do this. Maybe you catch a reflection of yourself in a store window. Maybe you see a bus going by. Perhaps you spy a dog on the street, or a pebble at your feet. It does not matter what you focus on for those ten seconds. Just stop for a tiny moment and appreciate that moment in a singular way.

Experience this while making love. Stop what you are doing for ten seconds, separate the moment into its component parts, select one part of the moment and peer deeply into it. Maybe it is the look in your beloved's eyes. Maybe it is a sensation you are feeling—or creating. Just stop for a tiny moment and appreciate that moment in a singular way.

I have regular times when I do this, and making love is one of them. Standing in the shower is another. Eating food is another. Pick up a pea from the plate, or a kernel of corn. Consider it. Appreciate it. Taste it utterly and completely. Your meal times will never be the same. Your showers will never be the same. Your lovemaking will never be the same. *You* will never be the same.

This is Stopping Meditation. It takes one minute a day. Sixty seconds, in six individual ten-second installments. Six moments within which you may produce The Holy Experience.

Today, stop what you are doing. Just *stop*. Look deeply into the moment. If nothing else, just close your eyes and focus on the sound of your own breath. Experience the pure energy of life moving into and through your body. Just for that moment, listen to yourself breathe. Watch yourself take deeper breaths. Just listening to yourself makes you want to go deeper into the experience—and so you begin to breath more deeply. It is a wonderful thing, an extraordinary thing. Just *stopping* makes you go deeper. Deeper into your experience, deeper into the mind of God.

Now here is a meditation program that I have recommended to many people: (1) Walking Meditation in the morning; (2) Stopping Meditation during the day, six times; (3) Sitting Meditation at night.

The purpose of all of these meditations is to create focus. It is about focusing your attention on your experience. The reason for focus: it allows you to be here now. Focusing on Now pulls you out of yesterday and out of tomorrow. You do not exist in those illusions. Your only reality is This Moment, right here, right now.

Peace is found in such awareness. As is love. For peace and love are one and the same, and you become one and the same when you enter into The Holy Experience.

Practice Stopping Meditation right now. It's simple, and it takes ten seconds. Right now, just . . .

Stop

And, after ten seconds, continue at . . .

WHO ARE YOU?

I had another wonderful teacher who showed me the *Who Meditation.* It goes like this. Whenever you are experiencing an emotion that you don't want to experience, just say, "Who?"

That's right. Just say to yourself, "Who?" Ask yourself, "Who is this here right now? Who is this that is having this experience?"

If you are alone, you can even turn this into a little chant. It can be very powerful. Just take a deep breath and, on the exhale, softly but powerfully chant: "Whoooooooooo?" Extend the vowel sound until you are out of breath. Then inhale and do it again. Do it three times. You will have slowed your vibration, and the invisible part of you will have a chance to "show up."

If you are not alone, but with another, or in some public place, you can do this little chant inside your head. Or you can just ask yourself the question I suggested above . . .

"Who is this that is having this experience?"

You can, of course, identify with any one of the number of "yous" that populate your inner world. There is the Little You and the Big You, the Injured You and the Healed You, the Scared You and the Brave You, the Powerless You and the Powerful You, the Worried You and the Confident You. But what I am hoping will happen, now that we've had this conversation, is that when you do the *Who Meditation*, you will chant yourself right into an awareness of your larger self, of your *true* self.

You are not a human being. You are not the person named John Smith or Mary Jones. You are not your body, you are not your mind, and you are not your soul. These are things that You have. The You that has these things—indeed, that has *given* your Self these things—is far bigger than any of them, and even all of them put together.

The You that you are is God, in Particular Form. You are Deity Individuated. You are an Aspect of Divinity. And so is everyone and everything else.

The whole realm in which you live and breathe and have your being is Heaven. The Kingdom of God is not something to which you are striving to return, but something within which you are living now. It is the place where you will be always, and all ways.

That kingdom has three realms: the Realm of Knowing, the Realm of Experiencing, and the Realm of Being. Your present consciousness is now focused on the Realm of Experiencing—otherwise known as the Realm of the Physical, or the Realm of the Relative. While you are here, you have all the tools you will ever need to *use* this realm to experience what you came here to experience . . . which is Who You Really Are.

You can not only experience it, you can recreate it anew as you go along, in the next grandest version of the greatest vision ever you held about that. That is the wonder of life and the glory of you.

This is, I know, a change in the way you have thought of yourself. It is a change in the way you have experienced your life. It is a change that will change everything.

Make this change permanent, not simply a temporarily held idea. Make it permanent now. For I tell you again . . .

. . . it is a change that will change everything.

"Go outside and play!"
said God.
"I have given you Universes as fields to run free in!
And *here*—take this and wrap yourself in it—
It's called: LOVE
and It will always, *always* keep you warm.
And stars! The sun and the moon and the stars!
Look upon these often, for they will remind you of your own
light!
And eyes . . . oh, gaze into the eyes of *every* Lover.
Gaze into the eyes of *every* other
for they have given you *their* Universes
as fields to run free in.
There.
I have given you everything you need.
Now go, go, *go outside*
and
play!"

—'*Go Outside and Play*' © 2007 Em Claire

AFTERWORD

Final Thoughts, but No Goodbye's

People who have read this material as an unpublished manuscript and others who have participated in workshops and spiritual renewal retreats where I have presented it verbally, have made a number of comments and asked several questions that have motivated me to clarify a few points in the "model" I am presenting here. I hope these Addendum Considerations will help "close the gap" for you, too, if you are querying these same things.

One question I have been asked is, "In the Line of Causality, what is the difference between 'belief' and 'truth'?" That is a very good question. My answer is that there is no difference in structure, only in source. Both one's "belief" and one's "truth" are *concepts*. Yet in the model I have been given to share, "belief" is understood to be a concept arising out of one's *perception*, while "truth" is understood to be a concept arising out of one's *data*.

Data is information pulled only from a person's past. It is information held in the mind. Perception is information pulled from a person's total view of life, which, in turn, arises out of that's person's perspective. If the person takes the soul's perspective—which includes information about the past, present, and *future*—rather than the mind's perspective, then Perception will always offer a broader view than simple Past Data.

I have also been asked how it can be said that "behavior" leads to "events" in every case in the life of people, as shown on my Line of Causality. "What about an elderly couple that I know," one lady challenged me at a workshop in Denver, "who was robbed at gunpoint in their own home and beaten badly by the men who broke in. How did this couple's behavior produce that event in their life?"

This has led me to further explore the Line of Causality and then explain it in deeper terms.

As I have come to understand it, the Line of Causality has two wild cards in it. These are Behavior and Event. I call these wild cards because their content can be placed in the Line of Causality in the singular sense (that is, by one person) *or in the plural sense* (that is, by the collective known as humanity).

Everything having to do with Perspective, Perception, and Belief is stuff that we, ourselves, as individuals, adopt for reasons singular to us. Then come Behavior and Event, which flow to each of us from our *own* Perspective, Perception, and Belief, *as well as those of others.*

Here in the Line of Causality there is a "seep through" or a "bleed through" from the life encounter of everyone in our environment. This bleed through plays a collective effect on the Behaviors and Events that we each individually encounter in life. This does not mean, however, that we do not control or create our experience and our reality. We still most certainly do, for after an Event occurs, the mechanism of the mind becomes a singularly influenced device once again, reverting to an individual's own Data, Truth, Thought, Emotion, and Experience, so to produce an individual's own Reality.

Thus it could be said that nothing in the Behavior of, say, Ronald Cotton (mentioned earlier in this book as the man mistakenly identified as a rapist) produced the Event of his having been incarcerated for eleven years. It was something in the collective Behavior of others that produced this Event. Yet after the Event occurred, he returned to his own very singular Line of Causality to produce his own Reality, in which he forgave his accuser and became friends with her, writing a book together about their experience. I venture to say that his Reality was influenced heavily by the perspective that begins his Line of Causality, and which produces his own perception or view of the world.

Having said that, I acknowledge that the model here is a work in progress. It is *ever changing*—which, of course, is not only incredibly appropriate for this book, but *the very point of it.* And it is not only the people in my Changing Everything workshops who offer me new insights and take me to new areas of inquiry. You, too, can do this—and I hope that you will.

Online at www.ChangingChange.net, you can call up this book paragraph by paragraph, line by line, click on any word or phrase, and post a question or an observation about it. Others who have selected the same portion of the text may have already posted there, or may do so in the future, making for a lively online discussion.

The idea is for this book to be *living literature,* not some stuck-in-concrete thesis that is presented and then goes unquestioned and unchallenged. I am excited about the Interactive Book concept, and hope that you are, too.

Now, I have been asked by many people, "How can I make the changes you have been suggesting here?" They want to know, "Where do I start?" They earnestly ask, "What should I be doing right now?" They hear the message, they see the destination to which it seeks to take them, but they don't know how to "get there from here."

To help you get going and keep moving on all this, we have developed the Changing Change Program. This is an extraordinary resource that will *walk you through*, step by step, the transformation of your own life.

The very first section of this program—*Getting Started*—is powerful enough to make real change visible in your life very quickly.

The program includes Here Is What You Can Do Now section; life-prodding questions; practical suggestions; mental, spiritual, and emotional tools; sure-footed guidance; and *even personal coaching* if you wish. PLUS . . . a way for you to turn what you've learned into learning for others. That is, a way for you to *pass it on.*

Now let me be clear about something. You do not need the Changing Change Program in order to implement the insights found in this text. This book gives you all the information you require to get started, explaining the Mechanics of the Mind and the System of the Soul and offering you an opportunity to experiment with them to see if they make sense and work for you. The Changing Change Program is a supplemental resource for those who really want to delve deeply into the kind of life this book describes, who really see all this—as my wife Em said at the outset—as a *practice*.

With or without the Changing Change Program, there are five things that I believe a person must do to successfully and powerfully implement the Nine Changes That Can Change Everything:

1. Desire Absolutely
2. Understand Thoroughly
3. Embrace Completely
4. Enact Consistently
5. Share Widely

1. You have to desire to change your life, and the way you *experience* your life, more than anything else in the world. Every creation of God begins with desire. The more powerful the desire, the more likely the outcome. Desire is an emotion—and emotion *is the creative force of the universe.* That it why it is so sad that so many people think that emotions are things over which they have no control. Deeply desire. That is the first step.

2. What is given to you here is a complete technology for altering your reality and changing the way you experience change—which means, of course, changing your life, because life *is* change and change *is* life. Study this book thoroughly. If there is any part of it you do not understand, go to www.ChangingChange.net and use the resources that have

been placed there to *help* you understand it. The Changing Change Process discussed in this book is not the only way to dramatically and wonderfully change your life, but it is a way. *Don't throw this way away.*

3. This is not about partial involvement here. I am reminded of the story of the chicken and the pig. They were walking down the road one day and they came upon a billboard that read: *Ham and Eggs—America's Favorite Breakfast!* The chicken turned to the pig and exclaimed, "Look at that! Doesn't that make you proud?" To which the pig replied, "Well, that's easy for you to say. For you it's partial involvement. For me, it's total commitment."

This is about total commitment. This is not about embracing a few of these concepts; this is about embracing *all of it.* The thing is, there is a linkage here. One thing leads to another and depends on it for the whole to make sense. You can't cafeteria-line your own transformation, taking a concept here and grabbing an idea there. This is the real meal deal.

4. Changing your life means changing your life; it does not mean deciding to change your life; it does not mean talking about changing your life or reading about changing your life. The Changing Change Process requires not only total embracing of the concepts here, but consistent and continual application of them, day in and day out, moment to moment. Now this could sound like an arduous undertaking, but it need not be. It can be (and, indeed, always winds up being) a pure joy. Yet you must know what it involves.

One day a guru was teaching his students, when a student said, "Master, you have been teaching us for months and none of us seem to be getting any closer to enlightenment. What does it take?"

The guru smiled and said, "You must take a sieve to the ocean and fill it with water."

The students did not understand. They grumbled, "This is not a real guru. Everyone knows you cannot fill a sieve with water. It runs right out. That's the problem with what he teaches, too. It sounds good, but it runs right out." So his students deserted him.

All but one. A young woman said, "Master, I know the problem is not in your teaching, but in my understanding. Help me to understand."

Filled with compassion, the guru replied, "Come with me." He took her to a store and bought a sieve. Then he took her to the shore. "Here," he instructed, "fill this sieve with water."

Eager to learn, she went to the water's edge and dipped the sieve into the water. But when she brought it to him, all the water had run out. He only smiled. "Fill the sieve with water," he said quietly, and so she tried again, knowing that he would not ask her to do something she could not do. But it was no use. She ran back to him as fast as she could with the sieve, but the water ran out.

"Fill the sieve with water," he said simply, and she tried once more, this time dipping the sieve and turning and running back to him so fast that she lost her breath. Still, no water remained in the sieve. "To *hell* with this!" she screamed then. "I'm *done* with this! I'm done with *this whole life* of being a *spiritual student!*" She threw the sieve fiercely into the air and stomped away.

"Wait!" the guru called. "Look."

The young woman turned just in time to see the sieve riding the ocean waves . . . then sinking beneath the surface and disappearing. The guru approached the student. "You cannot just dip in here and dip in there. This is not about dipping and running. You have to throw yourself in. You have to be totally immersed."

And the student understood.

5. The way to make it easy to get where you want to go is to travel with others who are also going there. You do not have to "go it alone." First you can *get* help, then you can *give* help, by joining an online community of people from all over the world who are going where you are going—and helping each other get there.

Em and I have created just such an online community. I have spoken about this several times in the text, and I will now mention it once again. It is the Changing Change Network, and it is located at www.ChangingChange.net.

Here you will find many resources that could serve you wonderfully in this moment and for a long time to come, including:

- Question & Answer section, where you can post any question that came up for you as you moved through this text and get an answer from members of the Changing Change Network.

- Personal Interactive Area, your private "desk," where you can move into a direct personal experience of this message through individual study online, tracking your encounter in your own online journal.

- Changing Change Message Board, where you can interact with others in the Changing Change Network, sharing comments and observations and both *offering* and *receiving* suggestions and support during life-changing moments.

- Video and audio clips from me about many subjects relating to the Conversations with God series of books, from which this text has emerged.

- An Additional Resource Section listing books, people, and organizations that can be of enormous assistance to those facing major changes in their lives.

- Articles of interest posted periodically, relating to some facet of the information found here.

- Schedule of all upcoming Changing Everything Workshops, and an opportunity to attend them at a discount as a member of the Changing Change Network.

- Network Support Center, where anyone can ask for information, assistance, references of books, or people or organizations that could make a life transition easier.

- Frequently Asked Questions (FAQ) and Additional Explanation Area, where material in this text is explored in even greater detail.

- "How I Survived the Big Change in My Life" area, where members of the network can post their own stories.

All of the above features are free. You may move into an even higher level of interaction by ordering the *Changing*

Change Workbook and Study Guide, available for purchase by Network members at the website, or, to get on the fast track, by enrolling in the fee-based Changing Change Personal Program—an eighteen-week online course which includes the *Workbook and Study Guide,* as well as other exercises, reading assignments, mental/spiritual projects to complete, daily life experiments, applications technologies, weekly questions to ponder (and answer), and inspirational excerpts from the 3,000-plus pages of the Conversations with God material, all packaged into three six-week Units, focused on the Mental, Physical, and Spiritual aspects of personal transformation. The Network also offers opportunities to receive personal spiritual coaching on the phone or by email as a supplement to the Program.

And, you can place into the Personal Program someone who is on the waiting list for a full scholarship by bringing them along with you through the I Want to Share project, the part of the Program that implements one of its core teachings: What you wish to experience yourself, give to another.

Here is what I know about all of this: We are all in this Moment of Change together. The work we are invited to do is *our* work, not just your work or mine. If we do this work of personal transformation together, we can transform not only ourselves, but the world entire. If we *only* transform ourselves but *not* anyone else, we will not have moved very far in what we came here to do. For we are all one (the very first message of *Conversations with God*). What we do for another we do for ourselves, and what we fail to do for another we fail to do for ourselves.

I do not lift up the Self if I lift up only the single part of the Self that I call "me." That is a start, and it is a good start, but it is only the beginning. In the end, if no one else is uplifted, I have healed but one of more than six billion parts. That is like trying to heal your body by healing a cell at the tip of your finger. It's a start. It certainly is that. But it is not the end of things.

That's why I like to say: "It's *our* work, or it *won't* work."

And now here's the good news. Healing is exponential. Energy moves not in a 1-2-3-4 progression, but in a 2-4-8-16-32 progression. Therefore, moving an entire culture to a new experience of itself is not only possible (and today, with the speed of communication, ever more so), but probable. That is, it is going to happen. The only question, then, is, *what kind of culture will we move to?* That is, *what is the future we are creating?*

Everything is already changing, and if we want it to change in the direction that we choose, *we have to change everything.*

So start with yourself, then touch others.

So here I've offered some final thoughts, but do not say goodbye. I sincerely hope you will use the many resources available to members of the Changing Change Network and that we can stay in touch. Just go to the website above and *interact* with us!

I also offer you here these additional resources:

www.EmClairePoet.com
The website of the poet whose works appear in this book

www.MaryOMalley.com
An amazing teacher and guide on the journey through life

www.NealeDonaldWalsch.com
The personal website of this book's author

www.cwg.org
The website of the Conversations with God Foundation

www.Free2BU.com
The website of the global educational movement based on the
messages of *Conversations with God*

I will close with items that are usually placed by authors in the
front of their books—my Acknowledgments and my Dedication.

These have been moved to the back in this text so that you
could get right into the conversation I wished to have with you,
without wading through a lot of front matter. My placement of
this material here does not, however, in any way indicate
reduced importance to me. I so deeply appreciate all those I
have acknowledged here, and my book dedication is the sincere
expression of a grateful heart.

ACKNOWLEDGMENTS

It is important to me that I publicly acknowledge the
breathtaking and experience-altering contributions that have
been made to my life by those whose work and teachings I have
studied deeply, some of whom I have had the honor of knowing personally. If any of the ideas found here are considered
valuable, it is not because I am in any way brilliant, but rather,
because I have been blessed to have been led to people of true
wisdom, searing insight, and breathtaking clarity, and am
standing on the shoulders of giants.

These include . . .

Alan Cohen
Rev. Terry Cole-Whittaker
Werner Erhard
Lyman W. Griswold
Jean Houston
Barbara Marx Hubbard
Gerald Jampolsky
Byron Katie
Ken Keyes, Jr.
Dr. Elisabeth Kübler-Ross, MD
Dr. Ilchi Lee
Eckhart Tolle
Dennis Weaver
Marianne Williamson

Now, having read this book, you have heard their words and their ideas flow to you, through me. It is impossible with so many teachers for me to be able to say in every case from which one a concept, an idea, or an inspiration came to me. I owe them all so very much, and I am deeply, deeply grateful.

I want to acknowledge as well, and in particular, Beth and Jerry Stark, my in-laws, who are two of the finest people I have ever had the privilege to know. Conspicuous in their kindness, gentle, sensitive, and caring in their treatment of everyone whose lives they touch, generous in their patience, expansive in their understanding, unending in their forgiveness and acceptance, these two wonderful people have inspired me to be a better person, not by saying that I might, but by showing how we all might. That they have raised a daughter, my wife, who is herself all of these things *magnified*, is living testimony to Who They Are.

DEDICATION

I know it is more or less de rigueur when books are being published for an author to acknowledge a life partner—but perhaps it is not so usual for an author to acknowledge every one of them. I must do so, because each of the ladies with whom I have been privileged to spend a goodly portion of this life has contributed enormously to my awareness, my understanding, and my growth. Even as I ask forgiveness for all of the errors that I made in their presence, I offer my profound thanks to each of them. You know who are you, and I would tell the world would it not unfairly invade your privacy. Thank you. For all you gave me, and for all you suffered as I tried so hard to grow up.

And now, thanks Bigger Than Thanks to the extraordinary woman who gives me the gift of her presence in my life…my wife and spiritual companion on this final leg of my journey.

My Beloved, My Other, I cannot hope to adequately describe the wonder of you, the joy that you bring to so many moments, the healing of your touch, the gentleness of your being, the brilliance of your mind, the hugeness of your heart, and, most of all, the deep, deep wisdom of your soul. As I share intimate and loving companionship with you every day, I am aware of the unbelievable blessing that is mine.

I dedicate this book to you
EM CLAIRE
for it is you who
CHANGED EVERYTHING

THE WORKBOOK AND STUDY GUIDE

The comprehensive *Changing Change Workbook & Study Guide* mentioned in the Afterword is a highly recommended addendum to this text. The *Guide* focuses on specific areas of life experience, offering exercises, experiments, assignments, study questions, and extended commentary. The intent of this supplementary book is to assist readers of this text in applying, *functionally*, the concepts explored here. A look at its Table of Contents provides a glimpse into how the *Workbook & Study Guide* extends the reach of the material:

Chapter 1: *Changing Sadness into Happiness;* Chapter 2: *Changing Reaction into Response;* Chapter 3: *Changing Fear into Excitement;* Chapter 4: *Changing Expectation into Anticipation;* Chapter 5: *Changing Resistance into Acceptance;* Chapter 6: *Changing Disappointment into Detachment;* Chapter 7: *Changing Enragement into Engagement;* Chapter 8: *Changing Addiction into Preference;* Chapter 9: *Changing Requirement into Contentment;* Chapter 10: *Changing Judgment into Observation;* Chapter 11: *Changing Worry into Wonder;* Chapter 12: *Changing Thought into Presence;* Chapter 13: *Changing a Time of Turmoil into a Time of Peace.*

The *Changing Change Workbook & Study Guide* may be ordered at www.ChangingChange.net.